A BIT
OF BASIC

This book is in the
ADDISON-WESLEY SERIES IN JOY OF COMPUTING

Thomas A. Dwyer
Consulting Editor

A BIT
OF BASIC

Thomas Dwyer

Margot Critchfield

University of Pittsburgh

Illustrations by

Margot Critchfield

ADDISON-WESLEY PUBLISHING COMPANY
Reading, Massachusetts • Menlo Park, California
London • Amsterdam • Don Mills, Ontario • Sydney

The language BASIC was developed at Dartmouth College by John G. Kemeny and Thomas E. Kurtz.
This book was reproduced by Addison-Wesley from camera-ready proof supplied by the authors. The book was designed by Nancy Ross McJennett, and set in Palatino.
The cover design and art are by Margot Critchfield.

Library of Congress Cataloging in Publication Data

```
Dwyer, Thomas A       1923-
   A bit of BASIC.

   (The Joy of computing series)
   Includes index.
   1.  Microcomputers--Programming.
2.  Basic (Computer program language)
I.  Critchfield, Margot, joint author.  II.  Title.
III.  Series:  Joy of computing series.
QA76.6.D88       001.64'24        80-11428
ISBN 0-201-03115-9
```

Copyright (c) 1980 by Addison-Wesley Publishing Company, Inc. Philippines copyright 1980 by Addison-Wesley Publishing Company, Inc.

ISBN 0-201-03115-9
CDEFGHIJK-AL-8987654321

Contents

PREFACE

The number of people who have had the opportunity to learn something about computers and computing has grown dramatically in the last few years, mostly through the efforts of educational institutions. Now that low-cost microcomputers are appearing in homes, schools, and small businesses at the rate of thousands per week, there will be an even greater number of intellectually curious people who'll want to investigate the mysteries of computing, both in and out of school.

Most of these newcomers will want to achieve more than a casual acquaintance with the ideas behind computing. They'll want to learn how to tap the full potential and power of these incredibly flexible machines. In particular, they'll want to enhance their understanding of what computers can (and cannot) do through direct, hands-on experience with computer programming.

One of the best tools developed to date for helping beginners achieve this goal is the high-level programming language BASIC. This is an English-like coding system that makes it easy to use and control computer systems. It allows one to interactively "feed" ideas into the machine in the form of computer programs—sets of instructions that tell the computer how to carry out the job at hand.

The name BASIC originally meant Beginners All-Purpose Symbolic Instruction Code, but today the language is used by professionals for a wide variety of serious applications. This book covers all of the fundamental features of BASIC as used on the latest machines. It also introduces a number of the recent extensions to BASIC that make possible such diverse applications as word processing, business record sorting, and computer graphics. The goal of the book is to show that today, more than ever, a bit of BASIC can go a long way.

Chapter 1 discusses the electronic hardware of microcomputers and larger time-shared computers, and illustrates how this hardware is used to get started in BASIC programming. A complete discussion of the key features (and use) of standard BASIC is then given in chapter 2 in the form of eight "hours" that can be used for classroom or self-paced study. Chapter 3 shows how to write programs that produce simple graphics, and also discusses the use of BASIC functions and BASIC arrays. Chapter 4 summarizes the latest features of extended BASIC, with examples based on the use of BASIC-PLUS, Microsoft BASIC, TRS-80 Level II BASIC, and APPLESOFT BASIC. Additional examples showing how to use the special graphics features of these last two machines are given in the final sections. The first three chapters of the present work are revised versions of material that first appeared in our earlier book, *BASIC and the Personal Computer*. The material in chapter 4 is all new.

The programs used to illustrate these ideas are taken from several fields, but no previous experience with computing is required. While some of the applications go beyond those usually found in introductory books, they can be mastered by anyone with the enthusiasm (and perseverance) of the amateur. Also, working with an idea on a computer is very different from just reading about it. In fact, anyone who explores the concepts in this book using a computer can expect to experience a new kind of human learning. Computer explorations combine the insights of do-it-yourself learning with the discipline of logical thinking.

In addition to supporting personal computing, this book will find use in introductory computing courses for both colleges and secondary schools. For this reason, a selection of project ideas has been given at the end of each chapter. Student projects make a good alternative to traditional testing as a way of determining grades in such a course. There are also a number of self-test sections in the book to help clarify new concepts as they arise.

The authors wish to express their appreciation to the many students and teachers who, along with Bill Gruener of Addison-Wesley, encouraged us to put together an introductory book of this kind. It was also Bill who provided the exactly correct title, and then proceeded to make the many wheels turn that are essential for converting a publishing idea into reality. Finally we thank all those innovative individuals in the computer industry (many of them unknown) who have turned the field upside down by daring to produce the amazing machines that now make convivial computing possible for everyone.

A BIT
OF BASIC

THE WORLD OF PERSONAL COMPUTING

1.0 INTRODUCTION

The world of personal computing is basically a friendly one, and no special credentials are needed to become part of it. While it's true that modern computer systems involve complex technologies and theories, their use is becoming easier all the time. This means that the mastery of personal computing can be based on the strategy of doing interesting things first, and then using the experience gained as the basis for more detailed study.

A key part of this strategy is to use a liberal dose of imagination right from the start. Computer amateurs aren't afraid to fantasize a bit, knowing that's where half the fun lies. Surprisingly, most early ideas of this sort have become reality: color graphics, computer music, computer robots, and even computers that "speak" (and in a crude way "recognize") English.

Does this mean that computers can eventually be used to do just about anything—including the making of human judgments? No. The diversity in personal computing, and the way so many different points of view have contributed to its growth, makes it clear how impossible (and undesirable) that would be.

Part of the reason for this diversity is that personal computing spans all ages. Grade school kids are contributing entries to "computer fair" contests

3

that have the judges scratching their heads. Popular magazines on the subject are found nestled between the textbooks of college students. And more than a few over-forty types report that they are caught up in an involvement that's like nothing they can remember.

While the exact future of personal computing is still an unknown, it's clear that variety will always be a key ingredient. For many, personal computing will be mostly a spectator sport. For others, it will become a powerful tool for exploring all kinds of new ideas. In either case, an excursion behind the scenes to see what's possible—which is where we're now headed—is worth everyone's while.

1.1   ABOUT THE WORD "COMPUTER"

It used to be that computers were easy to spot. They filled large rooms with tons of electronics, crammed behind complex panels dotted with blinking lights. They were understood by only a handful of people, they cost a small fortune, and they were used for the most mysterious of purposes.

But a lot has changed in recent years. Advertisements now proclaim the virtues of everything from "computer-controlled fuel-injection" car engines, to "digital computer displays" for clocks and ovens. And the number of "computer-controlled" game attachments for home TV is growing rapidly. It's reasonable to ask whether all these uses of the word computer mean the same thing.

While there's an element of truth in such popular usage, in many cases the word computer really refers to a special-purpose piece of hardware built for one task. In such instances, it would be more accurate to use the words "microprocessor", "logical circuit", or "digital control circuit". As a rule, consumer products don't qualify as full-fledged computers.

But there's an important exception to this rule: it's the device called the personal, general-purpose, programmable digital computer. As the words say, this is not a machine built for any special purpose at all. In fact it comes out of the factory just waiting to be told what to do—to be *programmed*. It's the closest thing to an "imagination extender" that's ever been invented.

Of course there are some additional questions that need to be asked. Do personal computers really work? Who can afford them? And if my resistance breaks down and I get one, what will it do?

Those are good questions, and the answers to the first two are easy: (1) yes, those made by reputable manufacturers work, and (2) you can buy a modest one for about the price of a component hi-fi system, or a complex one for the price of an automobile.

The third question takes a bit longer to answer. We'll begin by giving a brief overview of the components found in modern computers, and then show how these machines can be programmed using the high-level programming language BASIC. New ways of using this language to make a general-purpose computer do all kinds of special purpose things will then be introduced in each successive chapter. The topics covered range over many of the areas that underlie professional computing today.

Before getting started on this plan, it will be helpful to first explain some of the strange abbreviations and jargon used to describe computer systems. We'll do this in terms of personal computers, but most of the words apply to larger systems as well.

1.2   SOME EXAMPLES OF PERSONAL COMPUTING SYSTEMS; A BRIEF GUIDE TO COMPUTER JARGON

If you read the ads for personal computers or visit a computer store, you very soon run into a new vocabulary: RAM, ROM, BYTE, I/O, SERIAL, PARALLEL, CPU, VDM, ASCII, PROM, EPROM, CRT, — it's all very mysterious at first. Let's try to clear the air by looking at an example of a rather complete personal computing system to see what each of these terms means.

You'll notice that there are several components in our system which interconnect (that's why it's called a computer *system*). There are also alternatives for some of the components, which is why the phrase AND/OR appears on our diagram. (Of course if money is no problem, you can drop the OR).

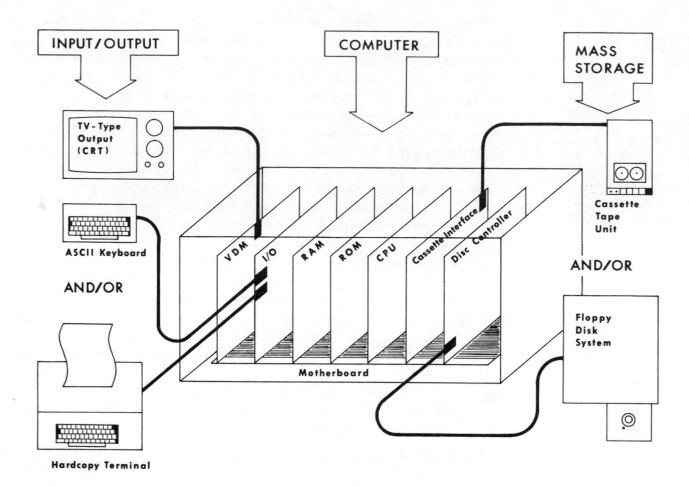

The three headings at the top of the diagram show that a full-fledged computer system consists of three major groups of components. We've labeled these as the INPUT/OUTPUT group, the COMPUTER group, and the MASS STORAGE group. Let's examine the components found in each of these groups in greater detail.

Input/Output Components

The INPUT/OUTPUT components are often called "I/O devices". An *input* device is used to transmit both programs and the data which are to be manipulated by programs *into* the computer. In other words, we want to take information in a form understood by humans, and feed it to the computer in a form that can be handled by machines. The most common input device is what's called an ASCII keyboard. This looks a great deal like a typewriter keyboard. It has all the letters, numbers, and special symbols needed to type programs, math formulas, and even English text. When a key is pressed on this keyboard, a unique "7-bit" code is generated. The word "bit" means a simple 2-valued piece of information (something like the "thumbs-up-thumbs-down" code of the Romans). In computer work the two values of a bit are written as 0 and 1.

For example when you press the key for the letter A, the 7-bit code 1000001 is sent to the computer. The process looks something like this:

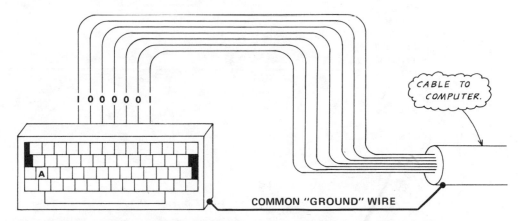

When each of the bits is sent on a separate wire as shown, we speak of a *parallel* connection. When the bits are sent one after the other on a single wire, the connection is called *serial*.

In the computer, bits are represented by two different voltages, usually called "high" (the 1) and "low" (the 0). The 1 and 0 can also be read as "bit on" and "bit off". The important point is that one bit gives only two different codes. We can come up with a lot more codes by using seven bits. With one bit there are $2^1=2$ codes. With seven bits we'll have $2^7=128$ codes, so we can take care of all the alphabet, numbers, and special symbols needed, plus a few extra codes for control functions.

OPTIONAL SELF-TEST:

For most programming, you don't have to know anything about the binary codes used in computers. This is all taken care of in the circuits inside the devices. Also, most manufacturers use the same code, so I/O devices can usually be interchanged between systems. The code used is called the *American Standard Code for Information Interchange*, or ASCII for short. The complete ASCII code is shown in Appendix B. Here are two questions about binary codes to try in case you can't wait until then.

1. Use Appendix B to translate the following imaginary conversation.

2. Radio amateurs often use a 5-bit code for transmitting messages. This means there should be $2^5=32$ different patterns of 0's and 1's possible. Make a chart showing all these patterns. If you need help, look at the hot dog problem in Section 2.4, where a 5-bit code is used (in disguise) for another purpose.

Output devices work in a reverse manner. Now the problem is to get the computer to display information in some kind of "human readable" form. For example, many personal computing systems use a TV monitor as an output device. This is either a slightly modified home TV set, or a closed-circuit TV monitor of the kind used in security systems. These are often called CRT displays (because they use *Cathode Ray Tubes*).

For TV output, a special piece of hardware is needed to convert the ASCII codes *inside* the computer back into symbols of the kind we use in ordinary printing (A,B,C,D,...,0,1,2,3,...,#,+,-,etc.). If you look inside the computer shown in our diagram, you'll see a "board" labeled VDM. This means *Video Display Module*. It's a circuit board that takes the ASCII codes from the computer, and converts them into dot patterns which show up on the TV monitor. (The term VDM-1 was coined by Processor Technology Company which made both boards and computers.) The patterns are chosen as shown in the accompanying photo to look like standard printing.

Another kind of I/O device is the "hard-copy" terminal. This includes both an ASCII keyboard for input, and a mechanism similar to that on an

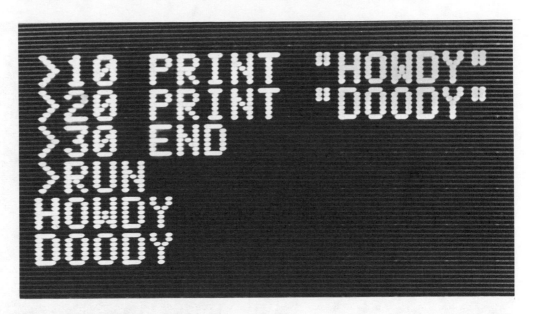

```
>10 PRINT "HOWDY"
>20 PRINT "DOODY"
>30 END
>RUN
HOWDY
DOODY
```

Dot patterns on a CRT screen produced by a video display module.

electric typewriter for output. So "hard-copy" means output printed on paper. This is important for applications where you want to save the output, or reproduce it (as done in this book). Hard-copy terminals do *not* need a VDM board. They contain their own code-conversion circuits. They are connected instead to what's called one "port" on an "I/O board". There are different kinds of ports for different kinds of terminals, but most modern I/O boards can be made to work with any kind of terminal. It's usually just a matter of changing a few wires on the board, following the instructions supplied by the manufacturer.

The Computer Components

The central part of our diagram is labeled "computer". This is shown as a collection of several circuit boards called *modules*. These plug into a common "motherboard". The motherboard has a bunch of printed wires (usually 100) soldered to connectors (called "slots") that accept the modules. This way a computer can grow. As you buy new boards, you simply plug them into an empty motherboard slot. So if you think you'll be expanding some day, it will be worth buying a computer that has a lot of slots available (up to 22 are available on some machines). You'll also want to make sure that the power supply (*not* shown in our diagram) which comes with your computer can handle that many boards. There is usually only one power supply, and it must have the capacity for handling all the boards plugged into the motherboard.

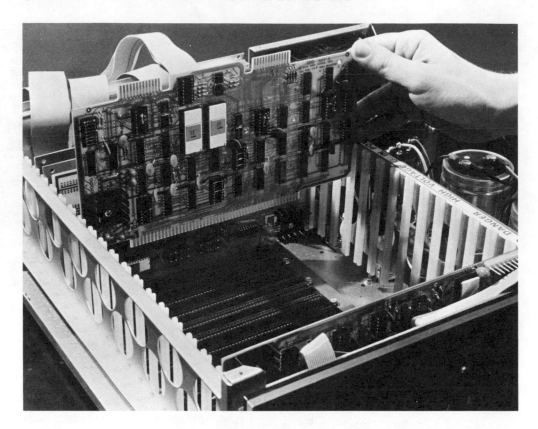

Microcomputer module board being plugged into a slot on the motherboard of an IMSAI computer.

One of the boards shown inside our computer is labeled RAM. This means it's a *Random Access Memory* board. It's where the programs and data we feed our computer are stored. This information is stored in binary form (all 0's and 1's). As a programmer in BASIC you won't have to worry about this since BASIC uses normal decimal notation.

Inside a microcomputer, the binary bits of information are usually organized in groups of eight, called *bytes* of memory. A small RAM board holds 4K bytes. Normally K means 1,000. But in computer work, 1K means 1024, so a 4K board has 4096 bytes. There are also boards with 8K, 16K, etc. bytes. Memory can be increased in computers by plugging in extra boards. The upper limit on many machines is 64K bytes which is 65,536x8=524,288 bits.

The reason these memories are called random (or direct) access is that the computer can go directly to any byte, either "reading" its contents, or "writing" (storing) new information there. The computer can rapidly access bytes of information at random—there's no need to sequentially search all through memory looking for something.

A ROM board contains *Read Only Memory*. Individual bytes of this memory can also be accessed directly (so you could also call it random access), but now no writing is permitted—only reading. ROM is used for permanent storage of programs or data that will never be changed Except—well there is a trick for erasing *some* ROM's with a special ultraviolet light. Then you can program new "permanent" data into them. Boards of this type are called EPROM boards, which means *E*rasable *P*rogrammable *R*ead *O*nly *M*emory.

The board labeled CPU (*C*entral *P*rocessing *U*nit) is where all the action takes place. The circuits on this board access data from memory, work on it, and ship it back out again. They also make sure the I/O devices get a chance to do their thing.

The heart of the CPU board is a microprocessor "chip", sometimes called a microprocessor unit (MPU). Some of the well-known microprocessor chips are the 8080 (Intel Co.) , the Z-80 (Zilog Co.), the 6800 (Motorola), and the 6502 (MOS Technology). The CPU board also contains "clock" circuitry to keep all this busy activity synchronized. The clock produces several million pulses per second, acting like a *very* fast orchestra leader working to keep everything in step.

The computer box (or "mainframe") also contains the I/O boards we've previously discussed, and the boards that may be needed to connect with mass storage devices. Let's see what these are all about.

Mass Storage Components

Imagine that you've had a busy session with your computer, and you now have a program for a brilliant new game up and running. But it's time to leave for a more gainful occupation, so you turn the computer off. Unfortunately, that act will wipe out all the information stored in RAM memory, so the next time you wish to use the computer you'll have to start all over. A similar problem occurs when you switch to a new program. The old one will have to be "scratched" (erased) before the new one can be typed in.

The solution to this dilemma is mass storage (also called off-line storage). The idea is to save copies of your programs and data in a form that can be re-loaded very rapidly—*without* re-typing at the keyboard.

The two most popular forms of mass storage are tape cassettes, and magnetic disks (sometimes spelled "discs"). The cassettes are the same kind as used in home recording. A special board inside the computer called the "cassette interface" is used to convert the bits in memory into a signal that can be fed into the recording jack of the tape recorder. This allows the *saving* of programs on tape. Conversely, the same board takes the output signal from your recorder (usually from the "monitor" jack), and converts it back into memory bits. This is how you *load* old programs back into memory.

An even better type of mass storage is the "floppy disk". This is about the size of a 45 rpm record, but the information is recorded magnetically.

The transfer speeds for disk are much higher than for tape. Further, disk playback machines can retrieve programs randomly. This is analogous to the way a person can pick up the arm on a record player and select one particular band of music (on tape you'd have to do a fast wind through everything). We'll have more to say about floppy disks and cassettes at the end of Chapter 3. We'll also mention a third type of storage, punched paper tape, in Section 3.8.

1.3 PACKAGED COMPUTER SYSTEMS

The previous section showed how a number of components are put together to make a full-fledged computer system. It's a bit like assembling a customized hi-fi system—confusing at first, but the most flexible route for those who want to experiment with all the possibilities of personal computing.

There are also computer amateurs who would rather concentrate more on applying their computer, and not have to worry about much more than plugging the system in and turning it on. There are "packaged" systems that allow one to do just that. At the high end of the price range, these take the form of desk-top computers made for commercial and educational uses. These systems are relatively expensive, and are sold mostly to institutions.

But there are also lower-priced packaged systems made for the consumer market, and the number is growing. Some are neatly enclosed in handsome cabinets with the keyboard built in. Others are a bit less pretentious, and assume you'll make your own enclosure. But most of them are both reliable and sophisticated.

An early example of a low-cost "almost" packaged system was the Apple I computer. It had all the circuitry on one board. This board included RAM and ROM memory, the CPU, I/O, a VDM, power supply, and even a tape cassette interface. This computer then evolved into the Apple II machine shown in the photo on the next page. The Apple II can produce color graphics as well as text, and we'll explain how this is done at the end of Chapter 4. It also has built-in expansion "slots" that allow the use of numerous special circuit boards, including some that can be applied to computer music and speech synthesis projects.

Despite their apparent simplicity, packaged computers allow the full range of programming. A typical session goes something like this:

1. Plug the system in and turn the power switch to ON.
2. Following a few simple directions, load the BASIC interpreter program from a cassette tape or disk. On many machines you don't even have to do this. BASIC is permanently stored in "read-only" memory.
3. Now type in the new BASIC program you've decided to try today. If you make a mistake, just re-type the incorrect lines.

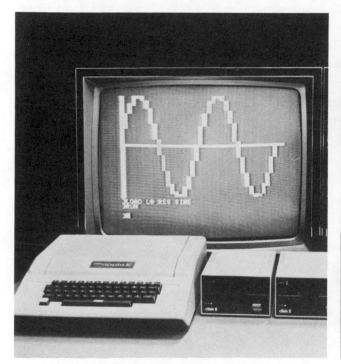

The Apple II computer.   The PET computer.

4. Run your program. If you don't like what it's doing, change it or add to it.
5. If you like what you see, save the program on a tape cassette to show your next visitor. Turn the power switch off.

The only things you may not have understood in the above were the references to "loading the BASIC interpreter", "typing in a BASIC program", or "running a BASIC program". So let's turn our attention now to the business of programming, and show some simple examples of what's involved.

1.4   A SIMPLE EXAMPLE OF PROGRAMMING IN BASIC

Once all the hardware is connected and working, it's time to say to our computer system "don't just stand there—do something." However we'll have to be a bit more explicit, and spell out that "do something" in greater detail. This means we're now ready to get into the business of programming, which isn't difficult if you use a high-level language. Actually, it's as simple as

ABC, where A means "get the machine ready", B is "write and load your program", and C is "run it".

Writing a program amounts to making a list of very exact instructions in a language "understood" by your computer. The fundamental language understood by any computer is called "machine language". This is not a good language for people however, so higher level languages like BASIC have been invented. Now the problem is that we'll need an interpreter—a special program that translates BASIC into machine language. BASIC interpreters are supplied by most companies that make personal computers. However these interpreters vary in sophistication, ranging from TINY BASIC to BASIC-PLUS. Some idea of how fancy your interpreter is can be gotten from how much memory it requires. You'll hear references to 4K BASIC, 8K BASIC, 12K BASIC, disk-extended BASIC, and others. In general, the larger versions are more powerful.

The Atari Computer has its BASIC interpreter stored on ROM in the form of a "cartridge" that can easily be inserted into the machine.

Now that we understand the need for an interpreter, we can get back to our ABC's of making a computer do something.

A. Get the machine ready. This means turning everything on, and then following the procedure needed to get your BASIC interpreter in memory. Each machine is different, so you'll have to read your instruction manual at this point. Also, some machines store BASIC permanently in ROM.
B. Write and load your program. How to write programs is the subject of most of this book. Once it's written (on paper), you load it by typing it in at the keyboard (if it's an old program, you load it from tape or disk).
C. Run (or execute) your program. This is easy. All you do is type RUN. If it works as expected, you jump with joy. If not (which is more likely), it's back to the drawing board in order to find your "bugs" (yes, it's probably your error). Actually, finding and fixing bugs is one of the more rewarding parts of beginning programming.

Incidentally, the total amount of memory you'll need will be that required by your BASIC interpreter *plus* that needed by your program. So if your computer has a total of 16K bytes of memory, and if you have an 8K BASIC, then your program will be limited to 8K bytes maximum. Most of the programs in this book will work within that limitation. To handle the larger programs, or to expand on them, a total of 32K bytes will be about right.

Here's what the ABC process looks like to the users of two typical machines. On the left you'll see a packaged system with a TV monitor for output and with BASIC stored in ROM. On the right a more complicated system is shown with a hardcopy output terminal, and a floppy disk for mass storage.

A. The BASIC interpreter is accessed from mass storage or from ROM.

BASIC is made available on the Apple II   BASIC is loaded from a floppy disk
by pressing the control and B Keys.   on the Altair computer.

B. A program is typed in which looks like this:

 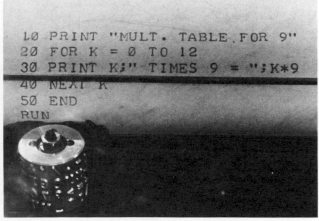

Program typed on the Apple.   Program typed on the Altair.

C. And now it's run

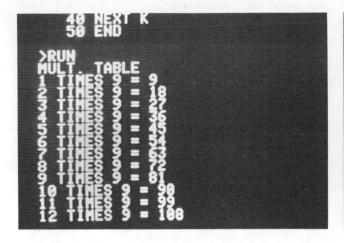

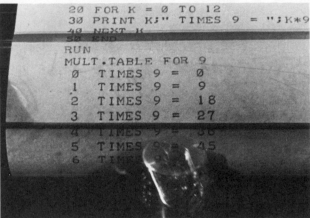

Run of the program on the Apple.   Run of the program on the Altair.

1.5 A CLOSER LOOK AT A PROGRAMMING SESSION

Now that we've got the big picture, let's zoom in on some of the details that steps B and C involve. Suppose you want to write a program to generate some multiplication tables (just in case your calculator breaks down some day).

If you only want to use the computer to calculate a few values, here's what you type (from now on, we'll only show hardcopy output, but of course the same ideas hold for TV monitor output).

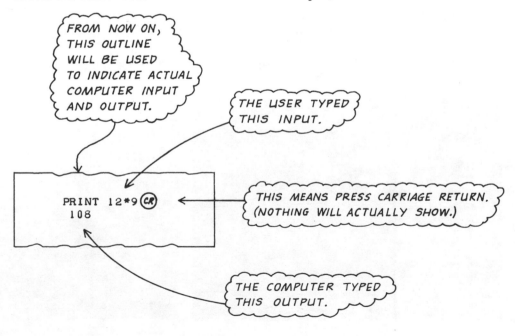

This example uses what's called *direct mode* (also called *immediate* mode) in BASIC. That's because you get an answer directly after you press "carriage return". (The carriage *return* key is always pressed at the end of lines.)

But this only gives us one multiplication. We could get two answers by typing the following direct mode statement:

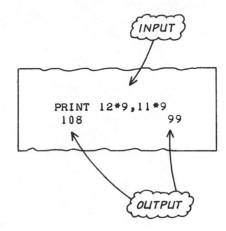

That's still not much of a multiplication table. It's time for a full-fledged *indirect mode* program. Here's what this might look like:

MULT TABLE

```
NEW

10 PRINT "MULT. TABLE FOR 9"
20 FOR K=0 TO 12
30 PRINT K*9
40 NEXT K
50 END
```

YOU TYPE ALL OF THIS. DON'T FORGET (CR) AFTER EACH LINE.

For reference purposes, we've called our program MULT TABLE. All the indirect mode programs in this book will be given a reference name which will be printed in the margin as shown.

Notice that an indirect mode program is made up of several "statements", each of which begins with a line *number*. (Don't worry too much about the details now—this will be explained again in Chapter 2).

So now we have a program, but no answers. That's because an indirect mode program doesn't run (or "execute") until we tell it to by typing the *command* RUN. Watch what happens:

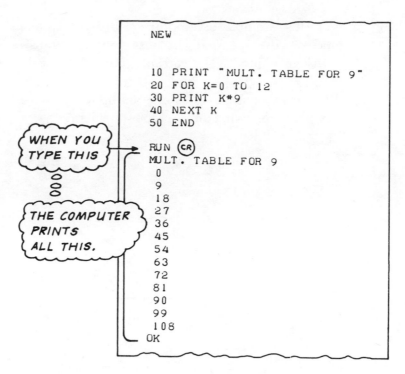

```
NEW


10  PRINT "MULT. TABLE FOR 9"
20  FOR K=0 TO 12
30  PRINT K*9
40  NEXT K
50  END

RUN ⓒ
MULT. TABLE FOR 9
   0
   9
  18
  27
  36
  45
  54
  63
  72
  81
  90
  99
 108
OK
```

WHEN YOU TYPE THIS

THE COMPUTER PRINTS ALL THIS.

As you can see, our program now produces 12 different products. To label them more neatly, all we have to do is change line 30 a bit. If we type in a new line 30 as follows, it will take the place of the old one. Then running the program will produce the improved output. (The improved output helps someone who doesn't know what our program is all about understand the results).

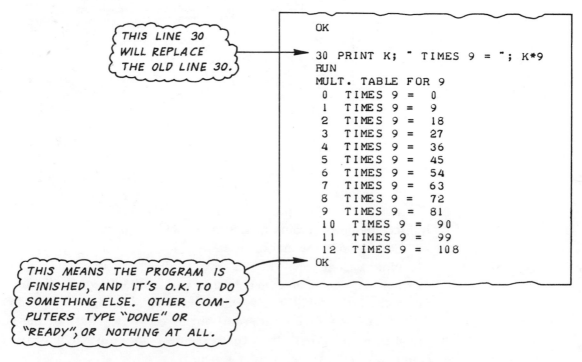

```
OK

30  PRINT K; " TIMES 9 = "; K*9
RUN
MULT. TABLE FOR 9
   0    TIMES 9 =    0
   1    TIMES 9 =    9
   2    TIMES 9 =   18
   3    TIMES 9 =   27
   4    TIMES 9 =   36
   5    TIMES 9 =   45
   6    TIMES 9 =   54
   7    TIMES 9 =   63
   8    TIMES 9 =   72
   9    TIMES 9 =   81
  10    TIMES 9 =    90
  11    TIMES 9 =    99
  12    TIMES 9 =   108
OK
```

THIS LINE 30 WILL REPLACE THE OLD LINE 30.

THIS MEANS THE PROGRAM IS FINISHED, AND IT'S O.K. TO DO SOMETHING ELSE. OTHER COMPUTERS TYPE "DONE" OR "READY", OR NOTHING AT ALL.

To see what the modified program looks like at any time, simply type the command LIST. This will give you a listing of all the latest statements in your program.

IMPROVED
MULT TABLE

```
LIST

10  PRINT "MULT. TABLE FOR 9"
20  FOR K=0 TO 12
30  PRINT K; " TIMES 9 = "; K*9
40  NEXT K
50  END
OK
```

If you want to see the output again, just type RUN. You can do this as often as you wish. To see the program, type LIST; to see it execute and produce output again, type RUN.

Incidentally, if you make typing mistakes, you'll usually get what's called an error message. This may not mean much to you at first, but the cure is simple: retype the offending line. Here's an example where the word RUN was typed incorrectly as RUNG. The computer called it a SYNTAX ERROR. Retyping the word correctly cured the problem.

Correcting an error by retyping a misspelled word.

You may now ask if we can extend this program to print several different multiplication tables. The answer is yes, and it only takes a few more lines. Project #2 at the end of this chapter shows how to do this.

1.6   ANOTHER EXAMPLE OF PROGRAMMING

Suppose that you've just finished the multiplication table program of the previous section, and want to try something else. You decide not to save your program because it's short and can be typed in again any time. For this reason, the first thing to do is to erase the old program from memory. In many versions of BASIC you do this by typing the command SCR (for scratch). Another form of this command is NEW, which means clear out memory because here comes a *new* program. (On a number of computers, you *must* type NEW at the beginning of any session. If you're not sure, try it. You won't hurt anything, but you *will* erase memory.)

Now let's enter a new program which is to calculate how much money will accumulate in a piggy bank. This time, we'll deliberately make some typing mistakes so you can see how this is handled.

PIGGY BANK

```
10 PRUNT "WHAT YEAR WERE YOU BORN";
ILLEGAL VERB at line 10

Ready

10 PRINT WHAT YEAR WERE YOU BORN;
SYNTAX ERROR at line 10

Ready

10 PRINT "WHAT YEAR WERE YOU BORN";
20 INPUT Y
30 PRINT "HOW MANY CENTS A DAY DID YOU SAVE";
40 INPUT C
100 FOR K=1 TO 21
110 PRINT Y+K, C*365*K/100
120 NEXT K
130 END
RUN

WHAT YEAR WERE YOU BORN? 1945
HOW MANY CENTS A DAY DID YOU SAVE? 75
    1946          273.75
    1947          547.5
    1948          821.25
    1949          1095
    1950          1368.75
    1951          1642.5
    1952          1916.25
    1953          2190
    1954          2463.75
    1955          2737.5
    1956          3011.25
    1957          3285
    1958          3558.75
    1959          3832.5
    1960          4106.25
    1961          4380
    1962          4653.75
    1963          4927.5
    1964          5201.25
    1965          5475
    1966          5748.75
```

THIS IS AN "ERROR MESSAGE". (PRINT WAS SPELLED WRONG.)

WE TRY AGAIN.

ANOTHER ERROR. (NO QUOTE MARKS.)

WE FINALLY GET IT ALL TYPED.

AND IT RUNS!

NOTE 1: When you type in two lines with the same line number, the old line is replaced. If you first type

    10 PRINT "HI"

and then type

    10 PRINT "HOWDY"

only the line 10 PRINT "HOWDY" is in the computer.

NOTE 2: To get rid of a line, just type its line number followed by a carriage return. Typing

    10 (carriage return)

will erase line 10 from the program.

NOTE 3: To get rid of an entire program type SCR or NEW. To double check on what's actually in the computer at any time, simply type LIST.

Suppose we now want to add a few additional lines to the output. Since the old program is still in memory, all we have to do is type in the desired new statements as follows:

IMPROVED
PIGGY BANK

```
50  PRINT "MONEY IN PIGGY BANK ON EACH BIRTHDAY --UNTIL 21"
60  PRINT "FROM"; C; "CENTS PER DAY, NO INTEREST"
70  PRINT "-YEAR-------TOTAL DOLLARS"

RUN

WHAT YEAR WERE YOU BORN? 1945
HOW MANY CENTS A DAY DID YOU SAVE? 87
MONEY IN PIGGY BANK ON EACH BIRTHDAY --UNTIL 21
FROM 87 CENTS PER DAY, NO INTEREST
-YEAR-------TOTAL DOLLARS
   1946            317.55
   1947            635.1
   1948            952.65
   1949            1270.2
   1950            1587.75
   1951            1905.3
   1952            2222.85
   1953            2540.4
   1954            2857.95
   1955            3175.5
   1956            3493.05
   1957            3810.6
   1958            4128.15
   1959            4445.7
   1960            4763.25
   1961            5080.8
   1962            5398.35
   1963            5715.9
   1964            6033.45
   1965            6351
   1966            6668.55
```

NOTICE THE ADDITIONAL OUTPUT.

Remember, the carriage *return* key must be pressed after every line *you* type, including the 1945 (year born), and the 87 (cents saved per day). Also remember that you are not supposed to understand how this program works — that's coming in Chapter 2. For now, the idea is just to get the big picture of how a programming session goes together.

Commands in BASIC

Words like RUN and LIST are called *commands*. Notice that they don't have line numbers. Also notice that commands cause something to happen right after you press the return key (CR).

There are several other commands in common use. For example, to store programs on tape or disk, there is usually a SAVE command. To retrieve a program, there is a LOAD command (on some systems, this is called the OLD command, since you're going to retrieve an old program). The SAVE and LOAD commands are not found in all versions of BASIC, so you'll want to check your system manual to see what commands are available.

All versions of BASIC have a command that "erases" the entire program currently in memory. On some systems the command is SCR (short for scratch). On others it is NEW (which means erase the old program, because I want to create a new one).

Some fancier versions of BASIC have a command called DELete for erasing groups of lines. For example,

DEL 50–70   or   DELETE 50–70

would delete *all* the lines with numbers from 50 up to (and including) 70.

1.7   HOW TO COPE WITH YOUR COMPUTER

By now it should be clear that no two computer systems will be exactly alike. The variety possible in components, together with the fact that the interconnections often have to be customized, means that many individual owners of computers will have unique systems.

Getting your own particular collection of hardware up and running can be both rewarding and frustrating. But help is available in the form of books, magazines, computer clubs, and computer stores. The better stores function something like a good high-fi shop, and offer both advice and service on the components they sell. They can also refer you to others who have put together similar systems, or to personal computing clubs where computer amateurs meet and share ideas.

The closest thing to a common link between the great variety of computer systems is the programming language BASIC. That's why most of the remainder of this book will explain applications in terms of BASIC programs. But even here you must expect some variation. Not all versions of BASIC have the same features. Also, the same features may produce slightly different results in output.

Don't let this discourage you. There's a very simple solution to the problem of adapting to such variations. It's to experiment. You'll be surprised at how good you can get at this (which really amounts to becoming your own teacher) once you see that experimentation won't hurt anything.

We'll try to help by pointing out some of the variations in BASIC as we go along. We'll also demonstrate some techniques for "simulating" fancy features you may not have in your version of BASIC. The best way to evaluate *any* BASIC is to try writing and running some of your favorite programs in it—to set up what are called "benchmarks".

One last suggestion—if you have a choice, get a BASIC that has (among other things) floating point arithmetic, arrays, and strings. Floating point arithmetic assures that you get full decimal values in your answers. For example, in some TINY BASIC interpreters, if you say PRINT 10/3 you'll get 3 for the output. A BASIC with floating point arithmetic will give an answer of 3.333333 which is of course much better (if not downright essential) for many applications.

As to what arrays and strings can do for you, Chapters 3 and 4 give lots of examples. Most versions of BASIC that take 8K bytes or more will have all these features. There's also little doubt that new and better versions will continue to appear. So it's a good idea to set one's sights high right from the beginning.

Timesharing

Using a language like BASIC means that the programs developed can be run on just about any microcomputer. But larger computers can also be used, since most of these can be programmed in BASIC. These machines are too expensive for individuals of course, so they are usually found at institutions where they are "shared" by many users. The technique that makes this possible is called *timesharing*. It works something like a very fast version of a telephone answering service where there is only one operator but lots of phones. Each client gets a fraction of the operator's time. In a similar manner, timesharing users only get a fraction of the computer's time, but the sequence repeats so rapidly there is usually no noticeable waiting for service.

To use timesharing you need a terminal with a keyboard for input, and either a typewriter-like printer or a TV-like screen for output. The terminal must be connected to the large computer either directly with wires, or indirectly with a gadget (called an acoustic coupler) that uses a regular telephone set to communicate with the computer.

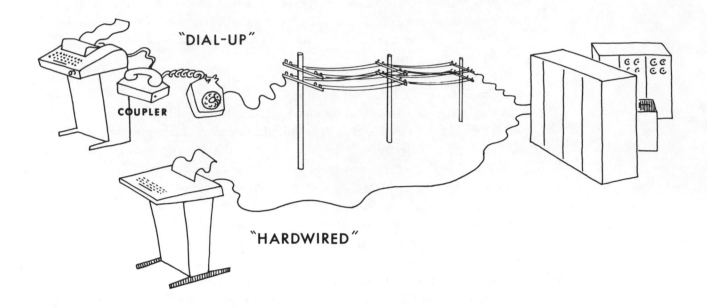

Once connected to the computer, people working at timesharing terminals can try most of the ideas about personal computing discussed in this book. When using BASIC, a timesharing terminal acts pretty much "as if" it were a personal computer.

There *is* one minor difference. Users of timesharing start their session by typing a line or two that gives their *user number* and their *password* (this is to control unauthorized use of the machine). This process is called "logging in". When finished, a timesharing user must also "log out". On many systems this is done by simply typing BYE (which means "goodbye"). An example of how this works for the timesharing system used on a PDP-10 computer is given in Appendix A. (Other systems will differ slightly, and local documentation should be consulted.)

1.8 PROJECTS

The last section in each chapter suggests some project ideas. These will usually be of enough substance to take a few days of on-and-off activity. By exception, we'll only suggest two short projects for Chapter 1. However they're well worth doing, since this will make the reading ahead much easier going.

1. Beg, borrow, or cajole use of a microcomputer that speaks BASIC, and
   actually type in and run the programs in Sections 1.5 and 1.6. Don't

worry about the fact that the way these programs work hasn't been explained yet. The main point is to get some hands-on experience with the whole process. The project will also get you familiar with the startup procedures needed for future programming.

2. After you have the multiplication table program of Section 1.5 running, try this more advanced version just to see what happens.

```
NEW
5 FOR D=1 TO 9
10 PRINT "MULT. TABLE FOR";D
20 FOR K=0 TO 12
30 PRINT D;" TIMES ";K;" = ";D*K
40 NEXT K
50 PRINT
60 NEXT D
70 END
RUN
```

The TRS-80 personal computer distributed through Radio Shack stores. With this machine use the ENTER key instead of CARRIAGE RETURN. The Level II BASIC supplied with this machine is very similar to BASIC-PLUS.

2
2
2
2
2
2
2
2

THE 8-HOUR WONDER
All About BASIC Programming
in One Long Day
(or Eight Short Nights)

GOTO

740 IF J >= 0 THEN 490

2.0 INTRODUCTION

Developing an artistic command of BASIC and extended BASIC — which is where we're headed next — will take a while. But getting the fundamentals under control takes very little time—even less than eight hours for most people. This is because the language has a small vocabulary, and the words used pretty well mean what you'd expect.

In this chapter we'll look at about twenty *key words* from this vocabulary. Another dozen or so key words will be explained in Chapters 3 and 4. These, together with a number of programming techniques, will enable you to express ideas with a growing fluency. Add the sage old advice of "practice, practice, practice", and you'll be a virtuoso of the ASCII keyboard in no time at all.

The key words of BASIC are used to make up what are called *statements* (which are something like "sentences" in the language). Statements are then put together to form *programs* . Here's a simple illustration of how this works for the example shown earlier in Chapter 1.

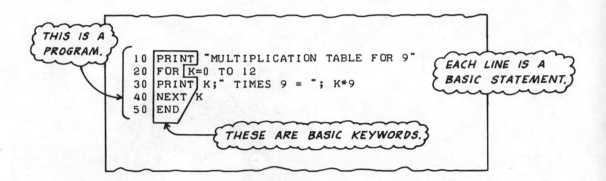

Each statement is an instruction to the computer. You'll notice that statements begin with what is called a *line number* (ln for short). This can be any integer from 1 to 65000 that *you* choose. The computer then uses the order of these numbers to determine the order in which to execute (carry out) the instructions in your statements.

Most programmers use line numbers 10, 20, 30, etc. to leave room for instructions they may have forgotten. For example, if you add a statement 35 at the bottom of a program like this:

```
    .
    .
    .
30 PRINT K
40 NEXT K
50 END
35 PRINT "*************************************"
```

the computer will know you want to print a line of asterisks after line 30. When you LIST this program, you'll find that statement 35 has been inserted between statements 30 and 40 (a very nice feature!).

HOUR 0: TEN WARM-UP EXERCISES

Before attacking the eight sections of this chapter and studying the details of how to write programs, it will be helpful to first try a few things informally. Readers who have had some experience with programming can skip this section. But if you're new at computing, spend as much time with these "warm-up" exercises as you wish.

The approach here will be to present the solutions to some simple problems of the kind that can be studied by imitation. It will soon become clear that most of these problems are not good examples of what computers can do. However the basic ideas shown in the solutions will be useful as later

building blocks. There won't be any detailed explanation of the key words used in this section. The idea is to invent your own explanations based on what happens. The formal explanations will be given shortly, at which time you can see how well your ideas hold up. Here's a brief guide to what the key words used in Chapter 2 are, and where the explanations will be given:

Key Words	Informally Used in Warm-Up Exercise	Explanation Given in Section
INPUT	5	2.1
PRINT	All Exercises	2.1
IF . . . THEN	10	2.1
STOP	10	2.1
GOTO	4	2.1
END	All Exercises	2.1
LET	1, 8	2.2
FOR . . . NEXT	6	2.3
TAB	— —	2.4
READ	— —	2.5
DATA	— —	2.5
RESTORE	— —	2.5
RND and RANDOMIZE	— —	2.6
ON . . . GOTO	— —	2.6
REM	— —	2.7
GOSUB and RETURN	— —	2.8
DEF FNK	— —	2.8
ON . . . GOSUB	— —	2.8

As the chart shows, we'll use about ten of the key words informally in the warm-up exercises. It is strongly suggested that you run each of the programs given in these exercises. This will be a good chance to become familiar with the keyboard and output screen (or paper) on your computer.

Also feel free to try variations on the solutions given. NOTE: Before typing in any of these programs, first make sure that the BASIC interpreter is loaded in your computer.

Exercise 1: Use your computer as a calculator.

Solution: There are two approaches you can try. The first uses *direct mode* (also called *immediate* mode). Try typing the following: (Some versions of BASIC do not permit direct mode. If this doesn't work go on to the indirect approach.)

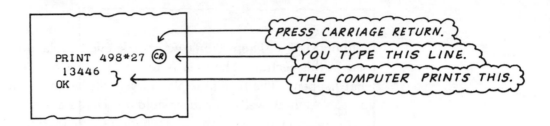

Direct mode statements do *not* have line numbers. Our example calculates the product of 498 and 27. To do this problem as an *indirect mode* program type the following:

PRODUCT

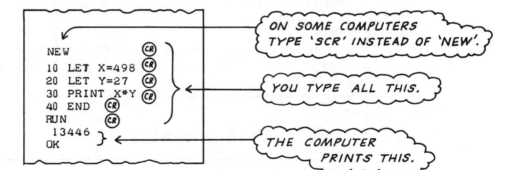

Notice that * means multiply. Similarly + means add, - means subtract, and / means divide.

     For this example, using indirect mode (with all those line numbers) is pretty silly. But as you'll soon find, it's the most powerful mode for more important problems.

Exercise 2: The restaurant bill for three people is $18.45, and they want to leave a 15% tip. Calculate how much each person should pay.

Solution: Using direct mode type this:

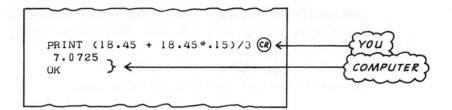

This tells us that each person owes about $7.07. Notice how parentheses are used to group the bill and tip together so that both are divided by 3. Using indirect mode, the program could be written as follows:

TIP

```
NEW (CR)
10 PRINT (18.45 + 18.45*.15)/3 (CR)
20 END (CR)

RUN (CR)
 7.0725
OK
```

NOTE: Users with a BASIC that doesn't have "floating point" (decimal) arithmetic will have to do everything with whole numbers as follows:

```
PRINT (1845 +1845*15/100)/3 (CR)
 707
OK
```

The answer is 707 cents (which is $7.07).

Exercise 3: Make the computer print some words—say, your name.

Solution: If your name is Bob, you could do this:

BOB

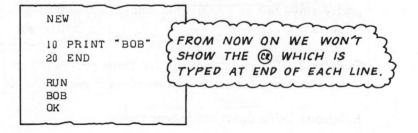

Exercise 4: That's not very impressive. Make the computer print your name lots of times.

Solution: That's easy. Watch closely.

BOB FOREVER

```
NEW

10  PRINT "BOB"
20  GOTO 10
30  END
RUN
BOB
BOB
BOB
BOB
BOB
^C  ←              THIS MEANS "CONTROL C".
BREAK IN 10
OK
```

This program will go on 'forever' unless *you* stop it by pressing "control C". That means holding down the key marked control, while you simultaneously press the key for the letter C. The 'break' message tells you at what line the program was interrupted. Your computer may not print this message. Also some systems use something different from control C for interrupting programs. Check your manual.

Exercise 5: Change the preceding program so it prints any name you wish.

Solution: You can do this by using the key word INPUT as follows:

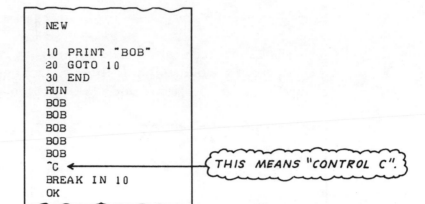

NOTE: ON SOME COMPUTERS THIS PROGRAM WILL NEED AN ADDITIONAL LINE — 5 DIM N$(30)

HI NAME

```
NEW

10  PRINT "WHAT'S YOUR NAME"
20  INPUT N$                        TYPE A SPACE HERE.
30  PRINT "HI ";N$
40  END

RUN
WHAT'S YOUR NAME
? JUNIPER
HI JUNIPER
OK

RUN
WHAT'S YOUR NAME
? NONE OF YOUR BUSINESS
HI NONE OF YOUR BUSINESS
OK
```

THE COMPUTER PRINTS EVERYTHING INSIDE THE DOTTED LINE. THE ? IS PRINTED TO TELL YOU IT'S YOUR TURN TO TYPE SOMETHING.

YOU TYPE THIS AFTER THE ? ALSO TYPE (CR).

Notice that you can RUN a program as often as you wish.

Exercise 6: Can you make the computer print lots of numbers— say, the squares and cubes of the first 50 integers?

Solution: The easiest way is to use the key words FOR and NEXT as follows:

SQUARES & CUBES

```
NEW

10  FOR N=1 TO 50
20  PRINT N, N*N, N*N*N
30  NEXT N
40  END
OK
RUN
 1              1              1
 2              4              8
 3              9              27
 4              16             64
 5              25             125
 6              36             216
 7              49             343
 8              64             512
 9              81             729
10              100            1000
11              121            1331
12              144            1728
13              169            2197
14              196            2744
15              225            3375
16              256            4096
17              289            4913
18              324            5832
19              361            6859
20              400            8000
21              441            9261
22              484            10648
23              529            12167
24              576            13824
25              625            15625
26              676            17576
```

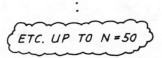

ETC. UP TO N=50

Exercise 7: You're a student, and your teacher wants you to calculate the number of square inches in pizzas of different diameters from 6 to 16 inches. But you only have 10 minutes before class.

Solution: Help is on the way. Try this:

PIZZA

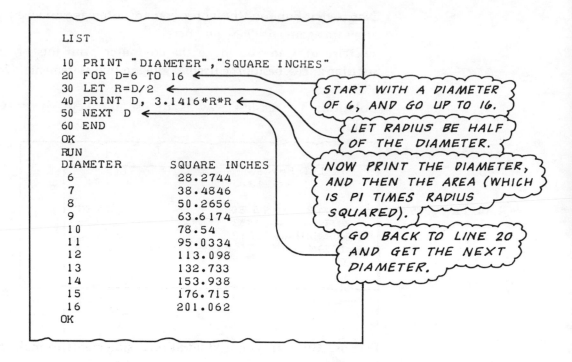

```
LIST

10  PRINT "DIAMETER","SQUARE INCHES"
20  FOR D=6 TO 16
30  LET R=D/2
40  PRINT D, 3.1416*R*R
50  NEXT D
60  END
OK
RUN
DIAMETER        SQUARE INCHES
  6                28.2744
  7                38.4846
  8                50.2656
  9                63.6174
 10                78.54
 11                95.0334
 12               113.098
 13               132.733
 14               153.938
 15               176.715
 16               201.062
OK
```

START WITH A DIAMETER OF 6, AND GO UP TO 16.

LET RADIUS BE HALF OF THE DIAMETER.

NOW PRINT THE DIAMETER, AND THEN THE AREA (WHICH IS PI TIMES RADIUS SQUARED).

GO BACK TO LINE 20 AND GET THE NEXT DIAMETER.

Exercise 8: You're doing a survey of voter preferences on a referendum and need to calculate percentages. How can this be done?

Solution: Here's one way. Let F mean 'number of votes *for* the referendum,' let A mean 'number of votes against,' and T mean '*total* number of votes.' Suppose there are 8,198 *for* , and 7,463 *against*. Here's a program to summarize the results and give percentages:

VOTE PERCENT

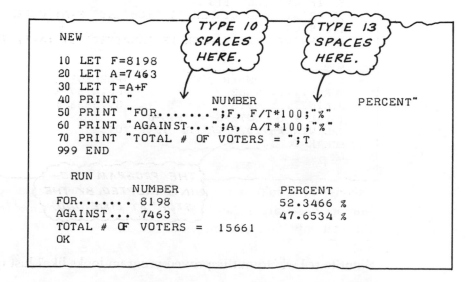

```
NEW

10  LET F=8198
20  LET A=7463
30  LET T=A+F
40  PRINT "          NUMBER              PERCENT"
50  PRINT "FOR......";F, F/T*100;"%"
60  PRINT "AGAINST...";A, A/T*100;"%"
70  PRINT "TOTAL # OF VOTERS = ";T
999 END

RUN
          NUMBER              PERCENT
FOR...... 8198               52.3466 %
AGAINST... 7463              47.6534 %
TOTAL # OF VOTERS =   15661
OK
```

TYPE 10 SPACES HERE.

TYPE 13 SPACES HERE.

Exercise 9: Suppose the votes had to be recounted. Can you run the same program again with new numbers?

Solution: Yes. You only need to change two statements. *Don't* type NEW (or SCR).

```
10  LET  F=9483
20  LET  A=6213
RUN
            NUMBER              PERCENT
FOR....... 9483                60.4167 %
AGAINST... 6213                39.5833 %
TOTAL # OF  VOTERS  =   15696
OK
```

Exercise 10: Can you add additional statements to make this program even fancier?

Solution: As long as you don't turn the computer off, or type NEW (or SCR), your program is still in memory. You can add new statements to the old program simply by typing them in. We'll illustrate this by adding an IF...THEN statement, a STOP statement, and two more PRINT statements as follows:

```
80  IF  A>F  THEN  110
90  PRINT  "THE  WINNER  IS  'FOR'  BY";F-A;"VOTES"
100 STOP
110 PRINT  "THE  WINNER  IS  'AGAINST'  BY";A-F;"VOTES"

RUN
            NUMBER              PERCENT
FOR....... 9483                60.4167 %
AGAINST... 6213                39.5833 %
TOTAL # OF  VOTERS  =   15696
THE  WINNER  IS  'FOR'  BY 3270  VOTES
BREAK  IN 100  ◄
OK
```

THE PROGRAM WAS INTERRUPTED BY THE 'STOP' AT LINE 100.

Want to see what your improved program looks like? Just type LIST.

VOTE WINNER

```
LIST
10 LET F=9483
20 LET A=6213
30 LET T=A+F
40 PRINT "              NUMBER                    PERCENT"
50 PRINT "FOR......";F, F/T*100;"%"
60 PRINT "AGAINST...";A, A/T*100;"%"
70 PRINT "TOTAL # OF VOTERS = ";T
80 IF A>F THEN 110
90 PRINT "THE WINNER IS 'FOR' BY";F-A;"VOTES"
100 STOP
110 PRINT "THE WINNER IS 'AGAINST' BY";A-F;"VOTES"
999 END
OK
```

That's a pretty fancy program, and it's time to start explaining how it (and the others in this section) work. So let's now look at the business of writing programs in more detail.

2.1   HOUR 1*: A PROGRAM TO HELP JUNIOR PASS ARITHMETIC 101

We'll start out by showing how to write a useful program with only six key words (in the case of IF ... THEN we should strictly talk about a key word "pair"). Our application will be an automated addition practice program that can be both a fun game to play and a painless way to get proficient at arithmetic.

To understand this program, we suggest you first look at what it does when it is executed (RUN). This is a good approach to most programming. It's better to first think about what you want to happen, and then write the program (set of instructions) to do it.

By looking at the RUN, you can see that the first thing this program does is to ask the person running it to type in two numbers. Then the program asks for the sum of these numbers. If the answer given is correct, the program prints TERRIFIC! Otherwise it prints NO, NO, NO followed by the right answer. The program also asks if another problem is wanted. Typing 1 means yes. Typing any other number (like zero) means no.

---

*Hour 1 is the longest since it has a lot of detail. It's probably best to go through it lightly the first time, and re-read it more carefully later.

HERE'S WHAT WE WANT FOR A RUN.

ADDITION PRACTICE

```
LIST
10 PRINT "ADDITION PRACTICE PROGRAM"
20 PRINT "TYPE IN 2 NUMBERS SEPARATED BY A COMMA"
30 INPUT A,B
40 PRINT "WHAT IS ";A;" + ";B;
50 INPUT X
60 IF X = A + B THEN 90
70 PRINT "NO, NO, NO ------ ANSWER IS ";A + B
80 GO TO 100
90 PRINT "TERRIFIC!"
100 PRINT "WANT ANOTHER (YES = 1)";
110 INPUT Y
120 IF Y = 1 THEN 20
130 PRINT "O.K. --- SO LONG."
140 END
```

AND HERE'S THE BASIC PROGRAM THAT MAKES IT HAPPEN.

```
RUN

ADDITION PRACTICE PROGRAM
TYPE IN 2 NUMBERS SEPARATED BY A COMMA
? 24,38
WHAT IS   24   +   38 ? 62
TERRIFIC!
WANT ANOTHER (YES = 1)? 1
TYPE IN 2 NUMBERS SEPARATED BY A COMMA
? 57,64
WHAT IS   57   +   64 ? 111
NO, NO, NO ------ ANSWER IS   121
WANT ANOTHER (YES = 1)? 0
O.K. --- SO LONG.
```

To explain how all this works we'll first explain each of the key words used. This will take a few pages, and will best be done with some simpler examples. Then we'll get back to the addition practice program and see how all the pieces fit together.

First the key words. We'll explain PRINT in a moment, but this will be easier if we first look at INPUT.

INPUT

In lines 30, 50, and 110 the key word used is INPUT. The idea of the INPUT statement is to make a program stop when it reaches that line, print a ? , and wait for the person running the program to type in (input) some "data". Data can be either numbers, or (as we'll explain later in Chapter 4), characters, or even "words". But for now they must be numbers, either integers (like 5, 89, -13) or decimal numbers (like 3.1416 or -.00328). *Fractions may not be used.* To input a number like 1/3, type .333333 instead.

INPUT is always followed by one or more *variable names* (separated by commas if there are two or more variable names). In our example, the variable names we have chosen in line 30 are A and B. To see what INPUT does let's look at a simpler program first:

INPUT

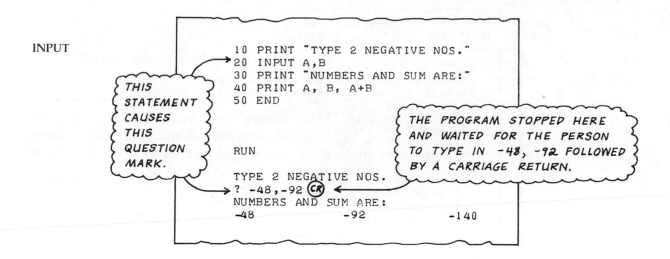

THIS STATEMENT CAUSES THIS QUESTION MARK.

```
10  PRINT "TYPE 2 NEGATIVE NOS."
20  INPUT A,B
30  PRINT "NUMBERS AND SUM ARE:"
40  PRINT A, B, A+B
50  END


RUN

TYPE 2 NEGATIVE NOS.
?  -48,-92 (CR)
NUMBERS AND SUM ARE:
-48            -92            -140
```

THE PROGRAM STOPPED HERE AND WAITED FOR THE PERSON TO TYPE IN -48, -92 FOLLOWED BY A CARRIAGE RETURN.

This INPUT statement causes the computer to print ? and then *wait* until the person running the program types two numbers and a carriage return. What happens inside the computer after the carriage return is pushed is that the two memory locations called A and B are set up, and the numbers -48 and -92 are stored in these locations. The situation looks something like the following:

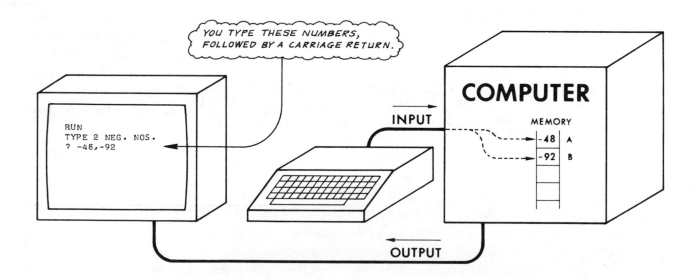

YOU TYPE THESE NUMBERS, FOLLOWED BY A CARRIAGE RETURN.

```
RUN
TYPE 2 NEG. NOS.
?  -48,-92
```

COMPUTER

INPUT

MEMORY

-48 A
-92 B

OUTPUT

When you type -48, -92, after ? mark, these two numbers are *input* to the computer's memory. (The computer also "echoes" them on the screen so you can see what you've typed.)

> NOTE: In our example two numbers had to be typed because the INPUT statement contained two variables. If it had only one variable (like INPUT A) then you would only type one number. If it had three variables (like INPUT A,B,C) then you would type three numbers, and so on.

Notice that the *name* of a memory location is different from the *contents* of that location. The name is often called a *variable name* (or simply a *variable*) because the contents can be changed (varied) by a program. Thus for each memory location, we can envision a picture like this:

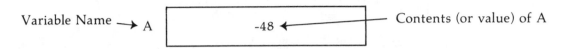

Variable Name ⟶ A | -48 ◀ | Contents (or value) of A

PRINT

If a program statement says: 5 PRINT "A" it means print (or display on a screen) the letter A. If a program statement says: 25 PRINT A it *doesn't* mean print the letter A, but rather to print the *contents* of memory location A (which is -48 in our simple example).

If a program says:

40 PRINT A,B,A+B

it means PRINT the *contents* of location A, the *contents* of location B, and the *sum* of the contents in location A and B. The *commas* in the PRINT statement mean that the contents (numbers, in our example) should be printed with enough space between them to make the numbers fall into *fields* that are 14 spaces wide. A space is allowed for the sign in front of the number, but + prints as a blank space. We used negative numbers so you could see the sign.

```
TYPE 2 NUMBERS
? -48, -92
NUMBERS AND SUM ARE:
- 4 8              - 9 2              - 1 4 0
```

0 1 2 3 4 5 6 7 8 9 10 11 12 13 14 15 16 17 18 19 20 21 22 23 24 25 26 27 28 29 30 31 32 33 34 35 36 37 38 39 40 41 42 43 44 45 46 47 48 49 50 51 52 53 54 55

Column Numbers

FIELD 1   FIELD 2   FIELD 3   FIELD 4

To make the numbers in a line of output print closer together, you can use a semicolon instead of a comma. Here's a simple test program that shows what happens:

OUTPUT
SPACING

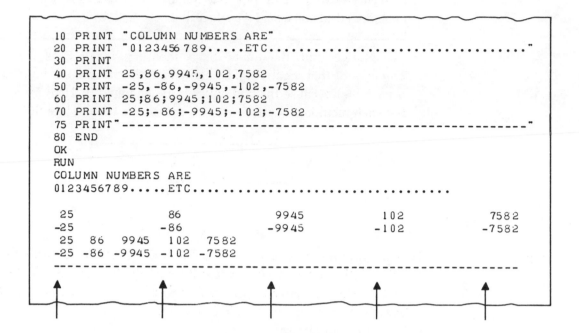

```
10  PRINT "COLUMN NUMBERS ARE"
20  PRINT "0123456789.....ETC....................................."
30  PRINT
40  PRINT 25,86,9945,102,7582
50  PRINT -25,-86,-9945,-102,-7582
60  PRINT 25;86;9945;102;7582
70  PRINT -25;-86;-9945;-102;-7582
75  PRINT"------------------------------------------------------"
80  END
OK
RUN
COLUMN NUMBERS ARE
0123456789.....ETC..............................

 25            86            9945         102          7582
-25           -86           -9945        -102         -7582
 25   86   9945   102   7582
-25  -86  -9945  -102  -7582
------------------------------------------------------
```

The arrows show where the fields caused by a comma begin. On a 70-column terminal, there are five such fields.

> NOTE: The spacing produced by the comma and semicolon in your BASIC may be different. To find out what they are, run the above test program and count what you get.

Notice that the "column" numbers used to describe positions across the output screen (or across the paper in an output printer) are numbered left to right starting with 0 (zero). Large printers can have 132 columns. Most printing terminals have 80 or 72 columns, while TV monitors may be limited to less (e.g. 40 columns). Also, some systems number the first column as 1.

TIME OUT FOR A SELF-TEST

The Self-Test sections in this book are meant to help you check your understanding of the more important ideas. The questions will be mostly in the form of "What does this program do?", or "Write a short program to do the following." These are meant to be pencil and paper exercises. But there will also be test items that say "Write and actually run a program to ... etc." This will usually mean several tries, since unforeseen errors (called "bugs") may creep in.

1. Pretend you're a "computer", and write down the output you would produce when commanded to RUN the following program. This is called "simulating" a computer RUN. It's a good way to check programs. An even better idea is for two people to swap programs they have written and simulate RUNS.

```
10 PRINT "TYPE TWO NUMBERS"
20 INPUT A,B
30 PRINT "SUM =";A+B,"PRODUCT =";A*B
40 PRINT "TYPE ANOTHER NUMBER";
50 INPUT C
60 PRINT "BET YOU CAN'T FIGURE WHERE"
70 PRINT "THESE NUMBERS CAME FROM"
80 PRINT (A+B)*C, A+B*C, A/B+C, A/(B+C)
90 END

RUN
TYPE TWO NUMBERS
?4,2
```

_____ ⎫
                                         ⎬ Finish the
_____ ⎭ output.

_____

2. Write a short program that asks for the dimensions (in feet) of a bedroom, living room, and den, and then prints the total number of square feet of carpeting needed.

3. Write and actually run a program that does the same as Problem 2, and also prints the number of square yards of carpet needed, as well as the total cost. (Note: you'll have to add an INPUT statement that requests cost per square yard.)

Let's now go back to our ADDITION PRACTICE program, and examine the output PRINT statements to see what else is possible. There are really five rules to remember about PRINT.

PRINT Rule 1   Anything in quotes is printed exactly as given when the program is RUN. Example:

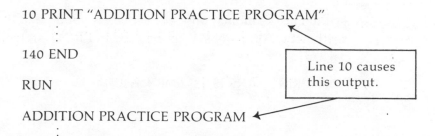

```
10 PRINT "ADDITION PRACTICE PROGRAM"
    ⋮
140 END

RUN

ADDITION PRACTICE PROGRAM
    ⋮
```

Line 10 causes this output.

PRINT Rule 2

When variable names appear in a PRINT statement (*not* in quotes), the contents of these locations are printed. For example, if A contains 47, the statement

    10 PRINT A

will cause the number 47 to appear on the output device (not the letter A).

PRINT Rule 3

You can mix these two kinds of output (called "items") in one PRINT statement. For example, if A = 24 and B = 38,

    10 PRINT "WHAT IS ";A;" + ";B

causes the output

    WHAT IS 24 + 38

A comma is used between items to place output in separate fields, usually 14 columns wide. A semicolon is used to cause items to print as close together as possible, but leaving a space in front for the sign of a number, and leaving one "trailing" blank after the number. If you want a spacing different from either of these, there is a special item called TAB that can be used in a PRINT statement. It will be explained in Section 2.4.

PRINT Rule 4

A semicolon at the end of a PRINT statement suppresses the normal carriage return (and line feed) that usually takes place automatically when the program is RUN. Look at lines 40 and 50 of the ADDITION program to see how this works:

    40 PRINT "WHAT IS";A;" + ";B;
    50 INPUT X

If the memory locations A and B contain 42 and 17 respectively, here's what we get when these two statements are executed.

    WHAT IS 42 + 17 ?

The question mark came from the INPUT X statement, but it did not appear on the next line because the normal carriage return was suppressed by the semicolon at the end of line 40.

PRINT Rule 5

Arithmetic combinations of variables and numbers (what are called "arithmetic expressions") can be used in PRINT statements. For example you can say:

    200 PRINT "ANS IS";3+(B*B-4*A*C)/4

The combination 3+(B*B-4*A*C)/4 is called an arithmetic expression. If A=5, B=10, and C=2, this statement will produce the output:

ANS IS 18

This is because
3 + (10 * 10 - 4 * 5 * 2)/4 =
3 + (100 - 40)/4 = 3 + 60/4 = 3 + 15 = 18

A Word About Extended BASIC

The explanations so far conform to the minimal standard BASIC defined by a committee of ANSI (American National Standards Institutes). However there are several implementations of BASIC that allow extra features. Two of the most powerful of these are BASIC-PLUS (Digital Equipment Corporation) and Microsoft Extended BASIC (Microsoft Company). The latter is now used by microcomputer manufacturers such as Radio Shack, Pet, Ohio Scientific, Exidy, Apple, SOL, Synertek, Rockwell, Atari, and several others. Microsoft BASIC is summarized in Appendix C. However there *are* a few differences in the way individual companies implement Microsoft BASIC, so you'll always want to check the reference manual for your computer. Project 4 on page 96 shows some of the differences between ANSI BASIC and extended BASIC. Section 4.1 shows how to translate some features of extended BASIC into minimal BASIC.

More About Expressions; Operations in BASIC

(a) In BASIC, you can form arithmetic expressions using five operators:

+ is used for addition
- is used for subtraction
* is used for multiplication
/ is used for division
↑ is used for exponentiation (some systems use **)

Exponentiation means "raise to a power". For example, 3↑4 means "3 to the fourth power" which is the same as 3*3*3*3.

(b) Expressions can contain both variables and numbers (called constants). Examples:

(1+2+3+4)/N
(A+4)/16-3.213*B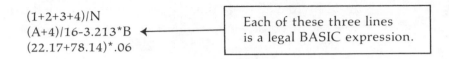
(22.17+78.14)*.06

> Each of these three lines
> is a legal BASIC expression.

(c) Parentheses are used in expressions to group things together and show in what order the operations should be done. For example

   (6+15)/3 means 21/3 = 7,
but 6+15/3 means 6+5 = 11.

When there are no parentheses, here are the rules the computer follows:

FIRST PRECEDENCE Exponentiations (if any) are done first.
SECOND PRECEDENCE Multiplications and divisions are done next.
THIRD PRECEDENCE Additions and subtractions are done last.
      All operations are done from left to right.
WHEN IN DOUBT, USE PARENTHESES TO CLARIFY YOUR MEANING.

TIME OUT FOR A SELF-TEST

1. Simulate running this program by completing the output.

```
10 INPUT A,B,C
20 PRINT A,B,C
30 PRINT A;B;C
40 PRINT "(A+B)*C = ";(A+B)*C
50 PRINT "THE";C;"TH POWER OF A+B IS";
60 PRINT (A+B)↑C
70 END
RUN
?20,-18,8
```

2. Write and run a program to convert a person's height into centimeters using the fact that 2.54 cm = 1 in. Here's what a run should look like:

```
RUN
TYPE IN YOUR HEIGHT (FEET, INCHES)?5,10
THANK YOU.
YOU ARE 177.8 CENTIMETERS TALL
```

Let's now explain the remaining key words used in our program.

END

The END statement is simple to use. It is *always* the last statement of any program, and it has no other parts except a line number. Many programmers use 9999 as the line number for END.

> *NOTE:* Strictly speaking, you don't even need the END statement in many versions of BASIC. But we recommend using it just in case you try running your programs on a computer system that requires it.

GO TO

This is also easy to use. It means that the "execution" of your program should depart from the usual rule of executing in the order given by the line numbers, and instead jump (GO TO) a specified line number. Compare these two examples:

```
10 PRINT 1          10 PRINT 1
20 PRINT 2          20 PRINT 2
30 PRINT 3          30 GO TO 10
40 END              40 END

RUN                 RUN

1                   1
2                   2
3                   1
                    2
                    1
                    2
                    .

                    .
                    . etc. (forever!)
```

The GO TO in the second example makes it go on "forever" (of course you can always pull the plug). This is called an "infinite loop". On many systems you can stop such loops by typing "control C" (which means hold down the key marked CTRL, and then also press the C key). A better way out is to use an IF...THEN statement, which we'll explain next.

One last comment. You can type either GO TO or GOTO. This is because BASIC ignores most spaces. However it's good to use spaces whenever they make programs more readable (to people, not computers). We'll have more to say about this at the end of Section 2.4.

IF...THEN and STOP

IF...THEN is a set of key words used in what are called "conditional branching" statements. Such statements are what make programs really interesting. To explain how this statement works, let's look at a simple example:

VOTING AGE

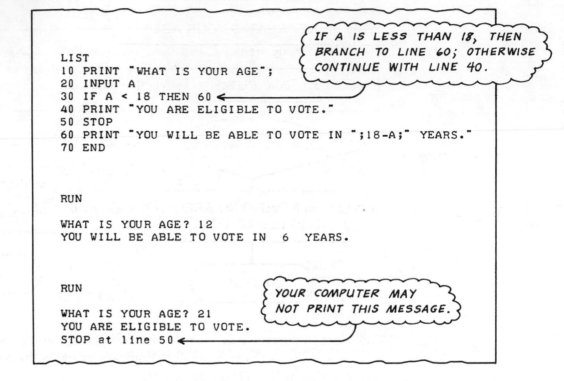

```
LIST
10 PRINT "WHAT IS YOUR AGE";
20 INPUT A
30 IF A < 18 THEN 60
40 PRINT "YOU ARE ELIGIBLE TO VOTE."
50 STOP
60 PRINT "YOU WILL BE ABLE TO VOTE IN ";18-A;" YEARS."
70 END


RUN

WHAT IS YOUR AGE? 12
YOU WILL BE ABLE TO VOTE IN  6  YEARS.


RUN

WHAT IS YOUR AGE? 21
YOU ARE ELIGIBLE TO VOTE.
STOP at line 50
```

IF A IS LESS THAN 18, THEN BRANCH TO LINE 60; OTHERWISE CONTINUE WITH LINE 40.

YOUR COMPUTER MAY NOT PRINT THIS MESSAGE.

Statement 30 is the IF...THEN statement. Here's what it means:

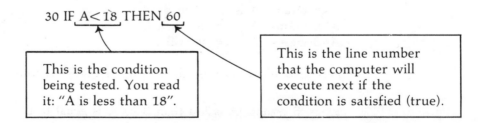

30 IF A< 18 THEN 60

This is the condition being tested. You read it: "A is less than 18".

This is the line number that the computer will execute next if the condition is satisfied (true).

"Satisfied" just means that it's *true*—A *is* less than 18. If the condition is *false* (not satisfied) that is, A is either equal to or greater than 18, then the computer will simply go on to the next statement. In our example it would go on to 40. The statement

    50 STOP

means that the computer is to stop executing the program at line 50—it should not go on to the END, but stop right where it is. You can have several

STOP statements in a program, but only one END, which *must* be the last statement.

We can illustrate the logical flow of this program with a diagram called a flow chart.

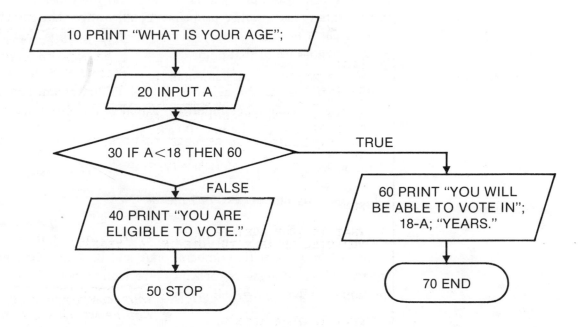

The most important box in our diagram is the diamond-shaped "decision" box, which shows the two possible branches or paths the computer can take. It represents the IF...THEN statement.

Here is how the various conditions are written in BASIC, using the relations $<$, $>$, and $=$.

A<B means "A is less than B".
A>B means "A is greater than B".
A=B means "A is equal to B".

You're also allowed to use the following combinations:

A $<=$ B means "A is less than B *or* A is equal to B".
A $>=$ B means "A is greater than B *or* A is equal to B".
A $<>$ B means "A is not equal to B".

One last (but very important) thing: the parts of a condition can also be expressions. All of the following are correct IF...THEN statements:

```
100 IF A+4 >A-B THEN 120
100 IF X<=B*B-4*A*C THEN 500
100 IF 3*X↑4<.0001 THEN 400
```

Relations have the lowest precedence. They are tested only after all expressions in the condition have been evaluated.

Meanwhile, Back at Our Main Example...

Let's now return to our ADDITION PRACTICE program, and show it in flow chart form. It has two conditional "decision" boxes, one to decide if the answer given to the problem is correct, and the other to decide whether the user wants to do another problem. You'll notice that the GOTO statement doesn't get a box. It's simply written next to the line that shows where the program "goes to" at that point.

Notice that line 120 branches back to line 20 for another problem only if Y=1. Any other number input for Y makes the program go to line 130. Some programmers write line 100 as:

100 PRINT "WANT ANOTHER (YES=1, NO=0)";

Of course, any number except 1 means "No".

The best way to follow this flow chart is to start at the top and trace the arrows. Choose specific numbers for A and B. Trace through the flow chart for two different answers for X, a correct one where X=A+B is *true*, and an incorrect one where X=A+B is *false*.

FINAL SELF-TEST FOR SECTION 2.1

1. Enter and actually RUN the ADDITION PRACTICE program. See if your favorite grade school student can use it, or even suggest some improvements.
2. Modify the program so it gives practice in multiplication.
3. Modify the program so it gives practice in adding three numbers at a time.

NOTE: In addition to the diamond-shaped "decision" box, flow charts use three other standard shapes. Trapezoidal-shaped boxes (slanted sides) are used to show both input and output. Sausage-shaped boxes are used to show the start and end of a flow chart. Rectangular-shaped boxes are used for most other things (LET statements, mostly).

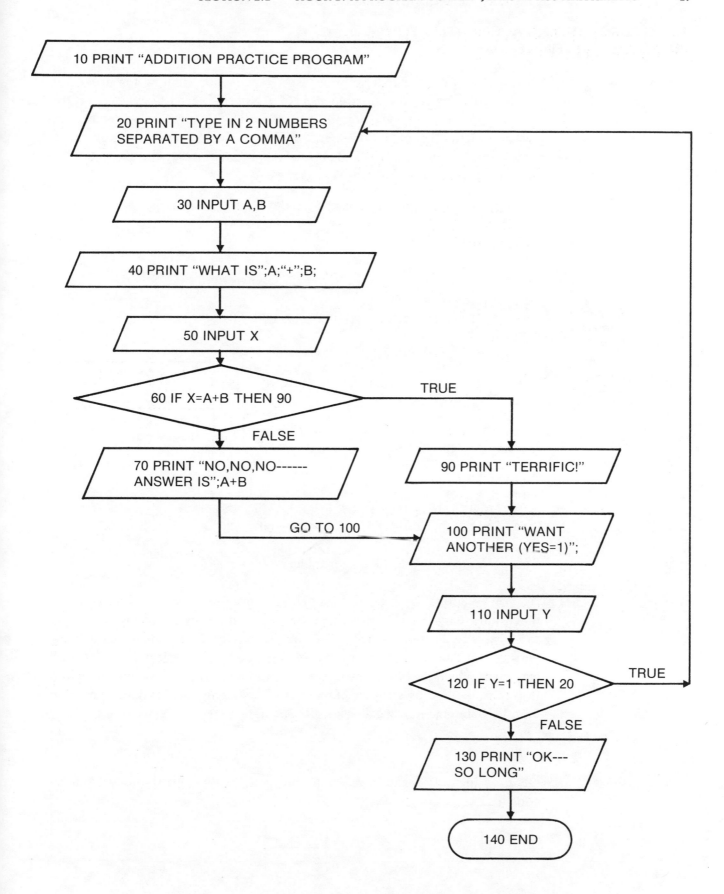

2.2   HOUR 2: ADDING A "COUNTER" TO YOUR
PROGRAM; PRINTING SCORES

The previous program required the "user" (the person running the program) to repeatedly answer the question WANT ANOTHER? This could get pretty tiring for someone who was training for an arithmetic quiz and wanted to do lots of practice problems. Here's a multiplication practice program that allows you to say how many problems you want right at the start. It also prints the percent of correct answers at the end.

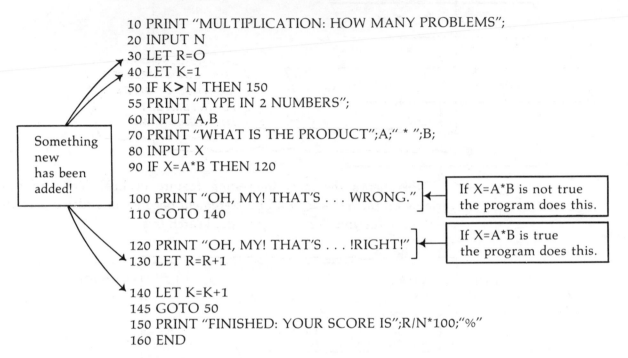

```
10 PRINT "MULTIPLICATION: HOW MANY PROBLEMS";
20 INPUT N
30 LET R=O
40 LET K=1
50 IF K>N THEN 150
55 PRINT "TYPE IN 2 NUMBERS";
60 INPUT A,B
70 PRINT "WHAT IS THE PRODUCT";A;" * ";B;
80 INPUT X
90 IF X=A*B THEN 120

100 PRINT "OH, MY! THAT'S . . . WRONG."      If X=A*B is not true
110 GOTO 140                                 the program does this.

120 PRINT "OH, MY! THAT'S . . . !RIGHT!"      If X=A*B is true
130 LET R=R+1                                 the program does this.

140 LET K=K+1
145 GOTO 50
150 PRINT "FINISHED: YOUR SCORE IS";R/N*100;"%"
160 END
```

Something new has been added!

This program uses a new key word, LET.

LET

As you've probably guessed by now, a computer program can't do very much until data has been stored in the proper memory locations. There are three ways to do this in BASIC. The first is an INPUT statement that let's the person running the program supply this data. The second is the LET statement which allows the program itself to load data in a memory location (the third method uses the READ and DATA statements explained in Section 2.5). LET statements are called *assignment* statements. The statement

```
10 LET  A=54
```

sets up a memory location called A and then "assigns" the number 54 as its contents:

An important feature of the LET statement is that the right side can be any arithmetic expression. For example here's a program that calculates the areas of circles with radii R supplied by the user:

CIRCLE AREA

```
LIST
10  INPUT R
20  LET A = 3.1416 * R * R
30  PRINT R, A
40  GO TO 10
50  END


RUN

?  1
   1                3.1416
?  10
   10               314.16
?  ^C
```

THE USER PRESSED "CONTROL-C" HERE TO INTERRUPT THE PROGRAM.

Now here's the most interesting feature of LET. You can have the variable on the *left* side of a LET statement become an updated version of its previous value given on the *right* side. Watch this:

COUNT

```
LIST
10  LET K = 1
20  PRINT K;
30  LET K = K + 1
40  IF K <= 10 THEN 20
50  END


RUN

   1  2  3  4  5  6  7  8  9  10
```

See what happened? K started out as 1. Then it was printed in line 20. Then, in line 30, K was changed to a 2 (a value equal to its previous value + 1). The IF...THEN in line 40 makes the whole process repeat until K is greater than 10.

Suggestion: you should always think of the LET statement as doing what's to the *right* of the = sign first, and *then* storing this value in the variable on the left side. Think of LET K=K+1 as meaning:

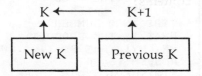

K ⟵ K+1

New K   Previous K

The above process is called *incrementing* K. In our case we increment by 1, but of course any increment could be used.

Now Back to the MULTIPLICATION PRACTICE Program

From the discussion of LET, you can now see how our MULTIPLICATION PRACTICE program works. K is a counter that keeps track of how many problems are done. When it finally becomes greater than (>) N, the number of problems which the user wanted to do, the program branches to line 150 and finishes up. Our other counter is R which keeps track of how many problems the user gets right. R only gets incremented (in line 130) if the answer X is correct (that is, when the condition in line 90 is true). This makes the program branch to line 120, followed by line 130 where the incrementing of R takes place.

The percent of correct answers is printed with the expression R/N*100 in line 150. For example, if you do 20 problems (N=20), and get 14 right (R=14), then R/N*100 = 14/20*100 = .7*100 = 70%. Here's a sample RUN of the MULTIPLICATION PRACTICE program:

MULTIPLICATION
PRACTICE

```
LIST
10 PRINT "MULTIPLICATION:  HOW MANY PROBLEMS";
20 INPUT N
30 LET C=0
40 LET K=1
50 IF K > N THEN 150
55 PRINT "TYPE IN 2 NUMBERS";
60 INPUT A,B
70 PRINT "WHAT IS THE PRODUCT ";A;" * ";B;
80 INPUT X
90 IF X = A * B THEN 120
100 PRINT "OH, MY! THAT'S .......WRONG."
105 PRINT "ANSWER IS ";A*B
110 GO TO 140
120 PRINT "OH, MY! THAT'S .......!RIGHT!"
130 LET R=R+1
135 GOTO 50
140 LET K=K+1
145 GO TO 50
150 PRINT "FINISHED:  YOUR SCORE IS ";R/N*100;"%"
160 END

RUN

MULTIPLICATION:  HOW MANY PROBLEMS? 3
TYPE IN 2 NUMBERS? 23,4
WHAT IS THE PRODUCT  23  *  4 ? 92
OH, MY! THAT'S .......!RIGHT!
TYPE IN 2 NUMBERS? 27,8
WHAT IS THE PRODUCT  27  *  8 ? 216
OH, MY! THAT'S .......!RIGHT!
TYPE IN 2 NUMBERS? 2,3
WHAT IS THE PRODUCT  2  *  3 ? 5
OH, MY! THAT'S .......WRONG.
ANSWER IS  6
FINISHED:  YOUR SCORE IS  66.6667 %
```

More About BASIC Variables

This is a good time to answer a question you may have had about what "names" can be used for BASIC variables. The answer is that in minimal BASIC a variable can be

(1) Any single letter, e.g., A, B, C, D, ..., Z.
(2) Any single letter followed by a single decimal digit, e.g., A1, A2, A9, B4, B7, Q7, Q8, Z0, Z3, Z4, Z5.

This means that there are 26 + 10*26 = 286 possible "legal" variable names (additional names for "string" variables will be introduced in Chapter 4.)

SELF-TEST

1. Which are legal variable names? X3, Z, 5K, AB, Q8, W-2, IOU

2. Simulate running this program and write down the output:

```
10 LET A=10
20 LET B=10
30 LET K=1
40 IF K > 5 THEN 100
50 PRINT K,A,B
60 LET A=A+2
70 LET B=A+B
80 LET K=K+1
90 GOTO 40
100 END
```

3. Write a program that acts like (simulates) an adding machine. A run should look like this:

```
RUN
ADDING MACHINE SIMULATOR
ENTER NUMBERS TO BE ADDED AFTER EACH?
ENTER 0 (ZERO) WHEN FINISHED
?142.83
?96.21
?895.04
?7.22
?0
THE NET SUM= 1141.30
```

Hint: Set up an "accumulator" variable for the sum with an initial value 0 (40 LET S=0). Then after you input each number(50 INPUT X), add it to the latest value in the accumulator (60 LET S=S+X).

4. Write and RUN a program to verify your checkbook balance. Hint: There's nothing to do! Simply use the above program, and enter deposits as positive numbers (?605.42), and check or bank charges as negative numbers (?-49.52).

2.3   HOUR 3: GETTING THE COMPUTER TO DO ITS OWN COUNTING; LOOPS

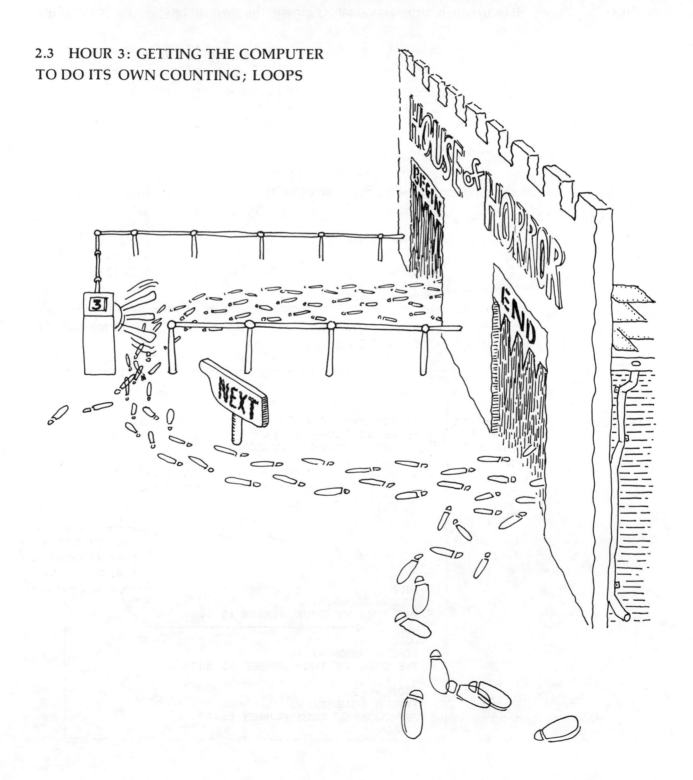

In the last section we showed the technique of using a counter together with an IF...THEN statement to control how many times a program executes a group of statements. This is called "looping" or "iteration", and it's an important type of control in programs. There is another way to control looping that is even simpler. It uses a pair of statements: a FOR statement together with a matching NEXT statement.

FOR...NEXT

Here are two programs that compare the two techniques for controlling loops:

Using a Counter

```
10 LET K = 1
20 IF K > 5 THEN 60
30 PRINT K; K*K; K*K*K
40 LET K = K + 1
50 GO TO 20
60 END
```

Using FOR and NEXT Statements

```
10 FOR K = 1 TO 5
20 PRINT K; K*K; K*K*K
30 NEXT K
40 END
```

Both programs produce the same output:

```
RUN
1 1 1
2 4 8
3 9 27
4 16 64
5 25 125
```

As you can see, the second program is simpler. Here's another example showing how several statements (called the *body* of the loop) can be controlled by FOR...NEXT statements:

SINGLE LOOP

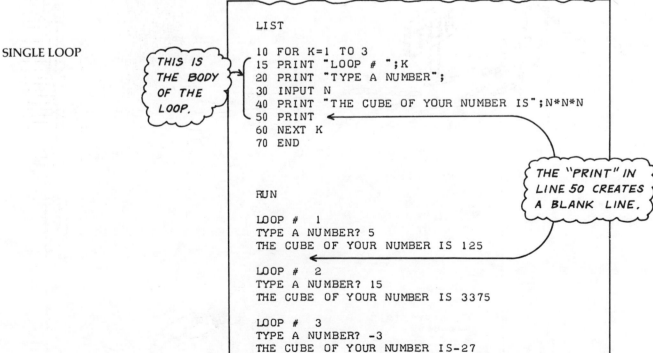

```
LIST

10 FOR K=1 TO 3
15 PRINT "LOOP # ";K
20 PRINT "TYPE A NUMBER";
30 INPUT N
40 PRINT "THE CUBE OF YOUR NUMBER IS";N*N*N
50 PRINT
60 NEXT K
70 END


RUN

LOOP #  1
TYPE A NUMBER? 5
THE CUBE OF YOUR NUMBER IS 125

LOOP #  2
TYPE A NUMBER? 15
THE CUBE OF YOUR NUMBER IS 3375

LOOP #  3
TYPE A NUMBER? -3
THE CUBE OF YOUR NUMBER IS-27
```

THIS IS THE BODY OF THE LOOP.

THE "PRINT" IN LINE 50 CREATES A BLANK LINE.

The full form of the FOR statement is

```
100 FOR K = 1 TO 25 STEP 5
——-(body of the loop)——-
200 NEXT K
```

The FOR statement really has three key words, FOR, TO, and STEP. The word STEP is used to say how much K should be incremented each time around the loop. If STEP is omitted, the STEP size (or increment) is taken to be 1.

Here's an example to show a negative STEP:

NEGATIVE STEP

```
LIST

10 PRINT "STAND BY FOR AIR TIME"
20 FOR K=5 TO 1 STEP -1
30 PRINT K;"SECONDS"
40 NEXT K
50 PRINT "YOU'RE ON!!"
60 END


RUN

STAND BY FOR AIR TIME
 5 SECONDS
 4 SECONDS
 3 SECONDS
 2 SECONDS
 1 SECONDS
YOU'RE ON!!
```

An important feature of the FOR statement is that variables or arithmetic expressions can be used after the = sign, and also after TO and STEP. Here's a simple example showing this feature:

STARS

```
LIST

10 PRINT "HOW MANY STARS DO YOU WANT TO BE PRINTED";
20 INPUT N
30 FOR K=1 TO 2*N
40 PRINT "*";
50 NEXT K
60 PRINT
70 PRINT "HA HA--THAT'S TWICE AS MANY AS YOU WANTED."
80 END


RUN

HOW MANY STARS DO YOU WANT TO BE PRINTED? 5
**********
HA HA--THAT'S TWICE AS MANY AS YOU WANTED.
```

SELF-TEST

1. Simulate running this program and write down the output you get.

   ```
   10 PRINT "IF JAN 1 IS A MONDAY THEN"
   70 FOR K = 1 TO 31 STEP 7
   30 PRINT "JAN";K;"IS A MONDAY"
   40 NEXT K
   50 END
   ```

2. Simulate running this program and write down the output.

   ```
   10 LET N = 10
   20 FOR K = 1 TO N STEP N/5
   30 PRINT K
   40 NEXT K
   50 END
   ```

3. Modify the MULTIPLICATION PROGRAM of Section 2.2 so that the number of problems done is controlled by a FOR...NEXT loop instead of the K counter.

2.4   HOUR 4: PRINTING PATTERNS; THE HOT DOG PROBLEM

Let's start by reminding ourselves of how to use a semicolon to keep printing on the same line, and how to use a PRINT to "undo" the effect of this semicolon. Look at the difference between these two programs:

```
10 FOR K = 1 TO 5          10 FOR K = 1 TO 5
20 PRINT "*";              20 PRINT "*";
30 NEXT K                  30 NEXT K
40 PRINT "FINISHED"        40 PRINT
50 END                     50 PRINT "FINISHED"
                           60 END
RUN
                           RUN
*****FINISHED
                           *****

                           FINISHED
```

In the second program, the PRINT in line 40 was needed to get a line feed and carriage return so that FINISHED appeared on a new line.

Now let's get fancy, and use two FOR loops, one inside the other. The second loop acts like the *body* of the first, and we say we have *nested* FOR loops.

DOUBLE LOOP

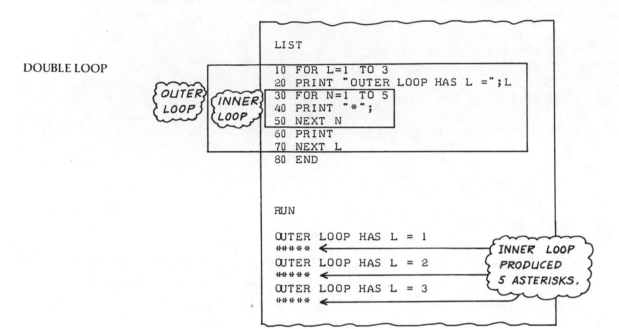

If you think through this program, you'll see that the body of the inner loop (which is simply line 40) gets executed 15 times. Looking at the asterisks printed should make this clear. The variable L controls how many lines get printed (3), while N controls how many asterisks per line (5), so 15 are printed altogether.

Programs with FOR loops can be made easier to read by using indentations that show the bodies of the loops. This will be illustrated at the end of this section. Another technique is to sketch in brackets or boxes that show the bodies of loops. RULE: Bracket or box lines showing the bodies of nested loops should *never* cross.

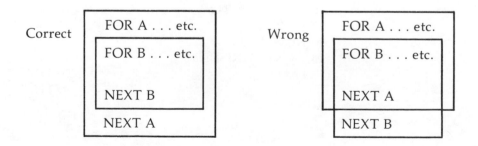

Could we have nested, nested FOR loops? You bet. Here's an example where N controls the number of asterisks per line, L controls how many lines, and B controls how many blocks of lines.

TRIPLE LOOP

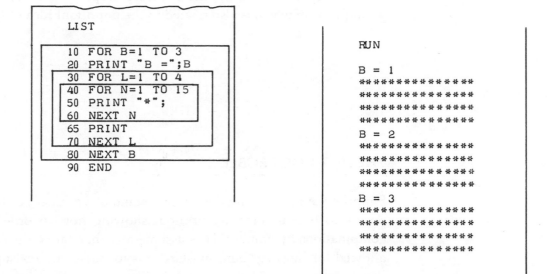

Here's a trickier version of the above which you should study carefully to make sure you understand what's going on.

VARIABLE LOOPS

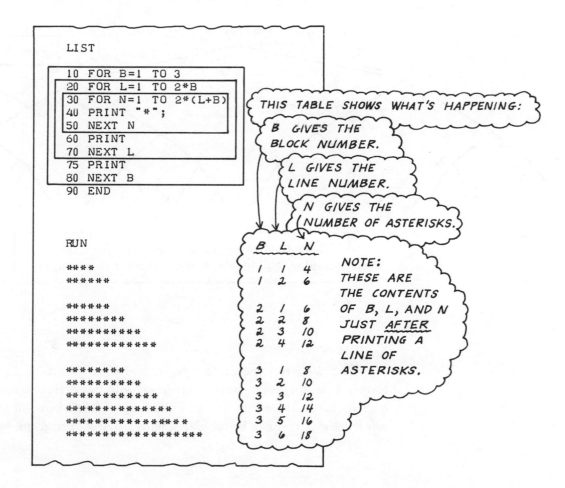

We'll return to the subject of printing patterns later, and show how to make them more interesting by using random numbers and other tricks.

Let's switch to another use of nested loops by showing an application to a fun problem which is also related to the important idea of *tree structures*.

THE HOT DOG PROBLEM

Suppose your're running the hot dog stand at your next club picnic, and you decide to post a computer printout showing how to order all the possible combinations by number. Let's assume that there are only YES/NO decisions allowed for hot dog, bun, mustard, mayonnaise, and catsup. To discourage overindulgence, we'll also print a calorie count for each combination.

The way to think about this problem is to picture what's called a *decision tree*.

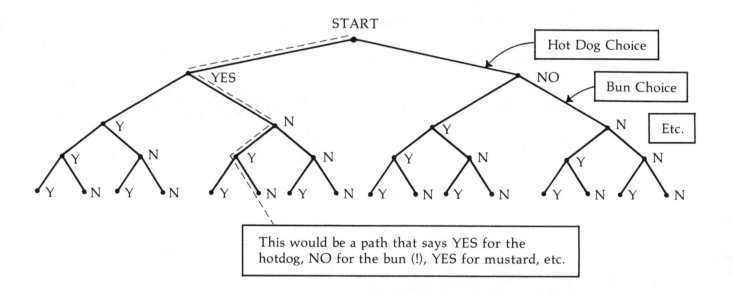

One way to generate a tree structure in BASIC is to use nested FOR loops, one for each level. Our tree will have five levels (one for each ingredient) so there will be five FOR loops. Here's how all the paths through our five-level tree can be tabulated with a BASIC program.

HOT DOG

```
LIST

10 PRINT "          DOG    BUN    MUST.    MAYO.    CATSUP"
15 LET K=1
20 FOR H = 0 TO 1
30 FOR B = 0 TO 1
40 FOR M = 0 TO 1
50 FOR Y = 0 TO 1
60 FOR C = 0 TO 1
70 PRINT "#";K;":   ";
80 PRINT H;"      ";B;"      ";M;"       ";Y;"      ";C;
90 PRINT "   CALORIES=";H*140+B*120+M*20+Y*100+C*30
95 LET K=K+1
100 NEXT C
110 NEXT Y
120 NEXT M
130 NEXT B
140 NEXT H
150 END

RUN
```

WEIGHT WATCHER'S SPECIAL

```
           DOG    BUN    MUST.    MAYO.    CATSUP
# 1  :      0      0      0        0        0       CALORIES= 0
# 2  :      0      0      0        0        1       CALORIES= 30
# 3  :      0      0      0        1        0       CALORIES= 100
# 4  :      0      0      0        1        1       CALORIES= 130
# 5  :      0      0      1        0        0       CALORIES= 20
# 6  :      0      0      1        0        1       CALORIES= 50
# 7  :      0      0      1        1        0       CALORIES= 120
# 8  :      0      0      1        1        1       CALORIES= 150
# 9  :      0      1      0        0        0       CALORIES= 120
# 10 :      0      1      0        0        1       CALORIES= 150
# 11 :      0      1      0        1        0       CALORIES= 220
# 12 :      0      1      0        1        1       CALORIES= 250
# 13 :      0      1      1        0        0       CALORIES= 140
# 14 :      0      1      1        0        1       CALORIES= 170
# 15 :      0      1      1        1        0       CALORIES= 240
# 16 :      0      1      1        1        1       CALORIES= 270
# 17 :      1      0      0        0        0       CALORIES= 140
# 18 :      1      0      0        0        1       CALORIES= 170
# 19 :      1      0      0        1        0       CALORIES= 240
# 20 :      1      0      0        1        1       CALORIES= 270
# 21 :      1      0      1        0        0       CALORIES= 160
# 22 :      1      0      1        0        1       CALORIES= 190
# 23 :      1      0      1        1        0       CALORIES= 260
# 24 :      1      0      1        1        1       CALORIES= 290
# 25 :      1      1      0        0        0       CALORIES= 260
# 26 :      1      1      0        0        1       CALORIES= 290
# 27 :      1      1      0        1        0       CALORIES= 360
# 28 :      1      1      0        1        1       CALORIES= 390
# 29 :      1      1      1        0        0       CALORIES= 280
# 30 :      1      1      1        0        1       CALORIES= 310
# 31 :      1      1      1        1        0       CALORIES= 380
# 32 :      1      1      1        1        1       CALORIES= 410
```

The output from this program would be a lot nicer if all the 0's and 1's (NO and YES decisions) lined up. We can make this happen by using the new key word TAB.

The statement 10 PRINT TAB (12) ;"*" will cause the "*" to print in column 12 (don't forget that columns are numbered from left to right starting with *zero*). We'll say more about TAB in Chapter 3, and show how using the form TAB(X) (where X is a variable in your program) can be used to produce graphical output.

To fix up our hot-dog problem all we have to do is change one line.

```
70 PRINT "#";K;TAB(5)":    ";


RUN
          DOG    BUN    MUST.    MAYO.   CATSUP
  # 1  :    0      0      0        0       0      CALORIES=  0
  # 2  :    0      0      0        0       1      CALORIES=  30
  # 3  :    0      0      0        1       0      CALORIES=  100
  # 4  :    0      0      0        1       1      CALORIES=  130
  # 5  :    0      0      1        0       0      CALORIES=  20
  # 6  :    0      0      1        0       1      CALORIES=  50
  # 7  :    0      0      1        1       0      CALORIES=  120
  # 8  :    0      0      1        1       1      CALORIES=  150
  # 9  :    0      1      0        0       0      CALORIES=  120
  # 10 :    0      1      0        0       1      CALORIES=  150
  # 11 :    0      1      0        1       0      CALORIES=  220
  # 12 :    0      1      0        1       1      CALORIES=  250
  # 13 :    0      1      1        0       0      CALORIES=  140
  # 14 :    0      1      1        0       1      CALORIES=  170
  # 15 :    0      1      1        1       0      CALORIES=  240
  # 16 :    0      1      1        1       1      CALORIES=  270
  # 17 :    1      0      0        0       0      CALORIES=  140
  # 18 :    1      0      0        0       1      CALORIES=  170
  # 19 :    1      0      0        1       0      CALORIES=  240
  # 20 :    1      0      0        1       1      CALORIES=  270
  # 21 :    1      0      1        0       0      CALORIES=  160
  # 22 :    1      0      1        0       1      CALORIES=  190
  # 23 :    1      0      1        1       0      CALORIES=  260
  # 24 :    1      0      1        1       1      CALORIES=  290
  # 25 :    1      1      0        0       0      CALORIES=  260
  # 26 :    1      1      0        0       1      CALORIES=  290
  # 27 :    1      1      0        1       0      CALORIES=  360
  # 28 :    1      1      0        1       1      CALORIES=  390
  # 29 :    1      1      1        0       0      CALORIES=  280
  # 30 :    1      1      1        0       1      CALORIES=  310
  # 31 :    1      1      1        1       0      CALORIES=  380
  # 32 :    1      1      1        1       1      CALORIES=  410
```

A Word About Programming Style

Programs should be easy to read. If would also be nice if they were interesting to read—if they had "style". Because of the limited vocabulary in programming languages, it's not too likely that many people will ever curl up in bed to read programs. But making them more readable is nevertheless an important goal. The "Little Book of BASIC Style" by Nevison is recommended as an excellent source of ideas on how to do this.

One technique is to use REMark statements that explain what's going on. Another is to use spaces and indentation. For example, it is helpful to indent the body of the FOR loop. When there are nested FOR loops, several levels of indentation are needed. For the hot dog problem, an indented version would look like this:

HOT DOG WITH TAB

```
LIST
110 PRINT "-------DOG----BUN---MUST.---MAYO.--CATSUP"
115 LET K=1
120    FOR H=0 TO 1
130     FOR B=0 TO 1
140      FOR M=0 TO 1
150       FOR Y=0 TO 1
160        FOR C=0 TO 1
170         PRINT "#";K;TAB(5);":   ";
180         PRINT H;"    "B;"     ";M;"        ";Y;"       ";C;
190         PRINT "    CALORIES=";H*140+B*120+M*20+Y*100+C*30
195         LET K=K+1
200        NEXT C
210       NEXT Y
220      NEXT M
230     NEXT B
240    NEXT H
250 END
```

Since it's difficult to type an indented version of a program, special "formatting" programs are sometimes used to do the indenting automatically. However you'll also find that some computer manuals advise *not* using indentation. The reason is that the extra spaces needed increase the size of programs, and also slow down their execution. So you'll see some microcomputer programmers going in the opposite direction, and writing things like this:

```
10FORX=1TON:PRINTX:NEXTX
```

This is efficient for the machine, but atrocious for human readers.

The programs in this book were run on microcomputers with limited memory, so fancy indentation wasn't possible. To improve readability, we've used balloons, brackets, and other extra notations instead. More complicated programs have been broken into segments which are distinguished by REMark statements with easily spotted dashed lines.

An example of using external brackets to distinguish the nested FOR loops in the hot dog problem is as follows:

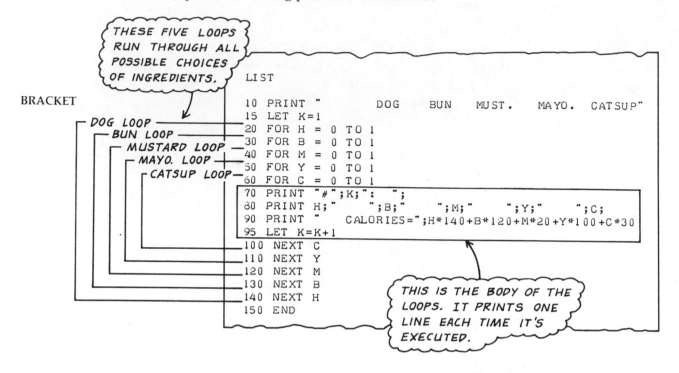

Programming with Style

An example of a program written with particular attention to style and readability is shown on page 145 as part of project 3. The programs in sections 4.2 and 4.3 of chapter 4 are examples of additional ways to style a program. As you start to write longer programs, it is recommended that you try your hand at developing a style of your own derived from these and other examples you have seen.

SELF-TEST

1. Simulate a run of this program:

```
10 FOR B = 1 TO 2
20 FOR L = 3 TO 1 STEP -1
30 FOR N = 1 TO B*L
40 PRINT "*";
50 NEXT N
60 PRINT
70 NEXT L
80 PRINT
90 NEXT B
100 END
```

2. Write and run a "hot dog" program that allows a triple meat choice of no-dog, beef frank, or kolbassi.

3. Write a program that uses nested FOR loops to print the multiplication tables for 7, 8, and 9. Here's a start:

```
10 FOR T = 7 to 9
20 FOR K = 0 TO 12
30 PRINT K; "TIMES";T;"=";K*T
40 ... etc. ...
```

4. (Optional) Read ahead to the chapter on strings, and see if you can make the hot dog program print words instead of numbers so the lines of output look like this:

28 : DOG   BUN   MAYO.   CATSUP   CALORIES = 390

2.5   HOUR 5: SHELF LABELS AND BATTING AVERAGES

The word is out. You're the first one on your block with a computer and the calls are starting to roll in. First the butcher, then the baker, and now—-the local sports writer. Seems he needs to crank out a list of batting averages fast, his calculator is broken, and he never did understand long division. Meanwhile, the corner grocer wonders if you could maybe print him unit-price tags of the kind used in supermarkets. Is there a simple way to handle both requests?

READ...DATA

One way to kill several birds with one stone in the world of computing is to realize that different programs may have similar structures, differing mainly in the data they use. For this reason, it would be nice if the data could be kept more or less separate from the program itself. This also makes it easier to expand or revise data later on. Here's how this idea works in BASIC for the batting average problem:

BATTING AVERAGES

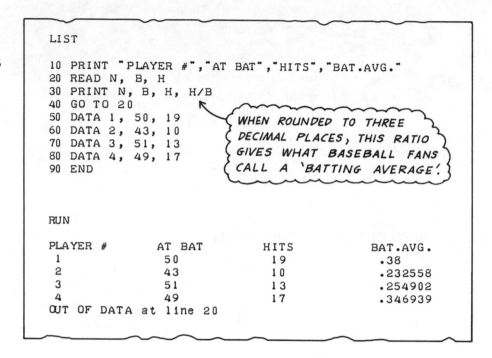

```
LIST

10  PRINT "PLAYER #","AT BAT","HITS","BAT.AVG."
20  READ N, B, H
30  PRINT N, B, H, H/B
40  GO TO 20
50  DATA 1, 50, 19
60  DATA 2, 43, 10
70  DATA 3, 51, 13
80  DATA 4, 49, 17
90  END
```

WHEN ROUNDED TO THREE DECIMAL PLACES, THIS RATIO GIVES WHAT BASEBALL FANS CALL A 'BATTING AVERAGE'.

```
RUN

PLAYER #        AT BAT        HITS        BAT.AVG.
1                 50           19           .38
2                 43           10           .232558
3                 51           13           .254902
4                 49           17           .346939
OUT OF DATA at line 20
```

When this program reaches line 20, it is told to READ enough data to load the variables N, B, and H. So it looks for a DATA statement (which it finds at line 50), and "uses up" the first three pieces of data it finds. You can think of what happens as follows:

20 READ N, B, H

50 DATA ①, ⑤⓪, ⑲

You should also picture this data as having been "used up":

50 DATA 1̸, 5̸0̸, 1̸9̸

The program next prints a line of output (line 30), and then does a "GO TO 20". This means it *again* reads data, but starting with the first "fresh" (unused) piece of data it can find. In our example, this is found at line 60, so the second time around our loop we have:

20 READ N, B, H

60 DATA ②, ④③, ⑩

This process continues until no more "fresh" data can be found, at which time an "out of data" message is printed. IMPORTANT: The data can be distributed over DATA statements any way you wish, provided it is in the *order* expected by the READ statement. For example, lines 50, 60, 70, and 80 could also be written as two statements:

        50 DATA 1, 50, 19, 2, 43, 10
        60 DATA 3, 51, 13, 4, 49, 17

or even as one statement:

        50 DATA 1,50,19,2,43,10,3,51,13,4,49,17

Actually, a program always treats all data as one big list. The READ statement simply goes down the list, "eating up" the data in "gulps". In our example, each "gulp" consists of three numbers, and it's *up to you* to make sure the groups of 3 correspond to N, B, and H.

Here's a similar program for our grocer friend. All we have to do is change our interpretation of what the variables mean, and use data appropriate to grocery prices. We'll also print things a little differently so the grocer can actually cut up the output to make shelf labels.

SHELF LABELS

```
LIST

5 PRINT "--------------------------------------------------------------"
10 READ N, Q, P
20 PRINT "PRODUCT #","QTY.IN OZ.","PRICE","UNIT PRICE"
30 PRINT N, Q, P, 100*P/Q; "CENTS PER OZ."
40 GO TO 5
50 DATA 1, 15, 1.29, 2, 4, .69, 3, 32, 2.49
60 END



RUN

------------------------------------------------------------------
PRODUCT #      QTY.IN OZ.     PRICE         UNIT PRICE
1              15             1.29          8.6 CENTS PER OZ.
------------------------------------------------------------------
PRODUCT #      QTY.IN OZ.     PRICE         UNIT PRICE
2              4              .69           17.25 CENTS PER OZ.
------------------------------------------------------------------
PRODUCT #      QTY.IN OZ.     PRICE         UNIT PRICE
3              32             2.49          7.78125 CENTS PER OZ.
------------------------------------------------------------------
OUT OF DATA at line 10
```

Improving These Programs

One of the nice things about writing programs is that once the basic idea is up and running, it's easy to add improvements. For example, both of the above programs suggest several kinds of additions. We'll describe five of these, and illustrate the last three.

(a) Limit the number of decimals to what people expect: .367 instead of .366666 for a batting average, 13.5 cents instead of 13.49999 for a unit price. There are two ways to do this. One uses the INT function which will be explained in Section 2.7. The other uses PRINT USING, explained in Chapter 3.

(b) It would be nice to have words or names printed instead of product or player numbers. The best way to do this is to use string variables, explained in Chapter 4

(c) It would be convenient to allow grocery data to be given in both pounds and ounces. This is easy to do. Here's one way:

20 READ N, L, Z, P

25 LET Q = 16*L + Z
    .
    .   ┌─────────────────────┐
    .   │ This means 15 oz. │
                             └─────────────────────┘
50 DATA 1, 2, 7, 1.31, 2, 0, 15, .89

┌────────────────────────────────────┐
│ We agree that this means product #1 │
│ contains 2 lbs. 7 oz. and costs   │
│ $1.31. Statement 25 then converts   │
│ Q to 39 oz.   │
└────────────────────────────────────┘

(d) The "out of data" message terminates the program. But suppose we want the program to continue and do other things? How do we handle this? (read on!)

(e) We may also want a program to re-use data that's been "scratched out". How do we "restore" such used-up data?

Here's a revision of the batting average program that answers both of these questions:

BATTING GRAPH

```
LIST

10  PRINT "PLAYER #   CLASS   AT BAT    HITS    BAT.AVG."
20  READ N, C, B, H
30  IF N = 0 THEN 110
40  PRINT N; TAB(10);
50  IF C = 0 THEN 90
60  PRINT   "VETERAN";
70  PRINT TAB(18);B;TAB(27);H;TAB(34);H/B
80  GO TO 20
90  PRINT "ROOKIE";
100 GO TO 70
110 RESTORE
115 PRINT
120 PRINT "BAR GRAPH OF PLAYER BATTING AVERAGES"
130 READ N, C, B, H
140 IF N = 0 THEN 220
150 PRINT "PLAYER #";N;
160 FOR K = 1 TO 100*(H/B+.005)
170 PRINT "*";
180 NEXT K
190 PRINT
200 GO TO 130
210 DATA 1,0,50,12,2,1,49,18,3,1,51,17,4,0,43,15,0,0,0,0
220 END
```

HERE'S WHERE THE DATA POINTER GETS SET BACK TO THE FIRST ITEM.

THIS EXPRESSION CONVERTS AN AVERAGE OF .24 TO 24 ASTERISKS, .367347 TO 37 ASTERISKS, ETC.

```
RUN

PLAYER #   CLASS   AT BAT    HITS    BAT.AVG.
   1       ROOKIE    50        12       .24
   2       VETERAN   49        18       .367347
   3       VETERAN   51        17       .333333
   4       ROOKIE    43        15       .348837

BAR GRAPH OF PLAYER BATTING AVERAGES
PLAYER # 1  ************************
PLAYER # 2  *************************************
PLAYER # 3  *********************************
PLAYER # 4  **********************************
```

In this program the data is read in groups of four. The second data item in each group of four is a code, with 0 meaning "rookie" and 1 meaning "veteran". For example, the statement

    DATA 1, 0, 50, 12

means that player #1 is a rookie (0) who was at bat 50 times and got 12 hits. Line 50 tests C to see what the code is, and then branches to the appropriate PRINT statement.

RESTORE

The revised batting average program uses the DATA in line 210 twice. The first time it's used to produce a table of batting averages. This is done in lines 10 to 100. This part of the program keeps looping back to line 20 to get new data. But the fifth time this happens, it finds the "phoney" data 0,0,0,0. We agree that storing a zero in N signals the end of data. The signal is picked up in line 30 which then causes a branch to the second part of our program (the bar graph routine from lines 120 to 200).

> IMPORTANT: Even though we only need one zero in N to signal end of data, it is essential that four zeros be put at the end of the data statement. This is because the READ statement has four variables to fill, and will squawk with an error message if it doesn't find four data items.

Now you can see what the special statement 110 RESTORE does. The first part of the problem "uses up" all the data. (What happens is that a "pointer" moves along the data to keep track, and when the pointer gets to the end of the list, the program knows it's "out of data".) The RESTORE statement resets this pointer back to the first data item. Now all the data can be used again. (Of course, re-running a program also resets the pointer, but that doesn't help in our example because we would never reach the bar graph part.)

SELF-TEST

1. Simulate running this program:

```
10 LET T1 = 0
20 LET T2 = 0
30 READ A, B
40 IF A = 0 THEN 90
50 PRINT A, B, A/B
60 LET T1 = T2 + A
70 LET T2 = T2 + B
80 GO TO 30
90 PRINT "TOTALS AND OVERALL RATIO"
100 PRINT T1, T2, T1/T2
120 DATA 6, 4, 10, 5, 4, 1
130 DATA 0,0
140 END
```

2. Write and run a program to help balance your checkbook. It should be like Problem 3 at the end of Section 2.2, but use READ and DATA instead of INPUT.

3. Write and run a student record program that has a DATA statement for each student in a class as follows:

100 DATA 101, 16, 75, 80, 65, 90

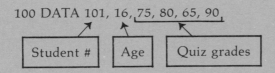

| Student # | Age | Quiz grades |

The program should print out a class roster with the grade average of each student. Finally it should print the average age in the class, the average grade for each quiz, and the overall class average.

2.6   HOUR 6: COMPUTER GAMES OF CHANCE

FLAVOR OF THE MONTH
RANDOM RAINBOW

"What a pity this isn't a sin!" Those are supposed to be the words of the novelist Stendahl upon tasting ice cream for the first time. They sound more like the utterance of a computer center director trying to find a rationale for evicting the game-playing devotees who clutter up his system.

But personal computers are a different story, and the wages of gaming on your own system are an intellectual refreshment that comes in more flavors than found in all the ice cream stands ever franchised.

This section explains the features of BASIC that help make this endless variety possible. We'll start by first answering one of the questions we raised in the last section: How do you make a number like

.343687 print as .344 ?
or .264689 print as 26.46 ?
or .891246 print as 89 ?

INT

One way to control the number of decimal places in a number is to use the INT function of BASIC. If a statement says

10 LET Y = INT(X)

the INT(X) part means that X is to be first "processed" by something called the INT (integer) function. What comes out of the processing is the integer just to the *left* of X on the number scale. Here are some examples:

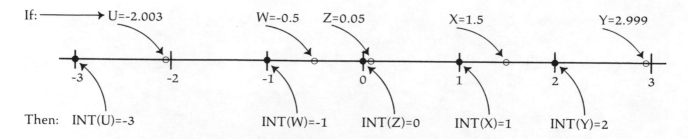

The following program shows some more examples of the differences between X and INT(X)

INT DEMO

```
LIST

5 PRINT "X", "INT(X)", "X/3", "INT(100*X/3)"
10 FOR X = -2 TO 2 STEP .5
20 PRINT X, INT(X), X/3, INT(100*X/3)
30 NEXT X
40 END



RUN

X                    INT(X)           X/3              INT(100*X/3)
-2                   -2               -.666667         -67
-1.5                 -2               -.5              -50
-1                   -1               -.333333         -34
-.5                  -1               -.166667         -17
 0                    0                0                0
 .5                   0                .166667          16
 1                    1                .333333          33
 1.5                  1                .5               50
 2                    2                .666667          66
```

To use INT for getting an answer in dollars and cents with only 2 decimal places (remember the UNIT PRICE program?) we can use the expression INT(100*X)/100. That's because

if	$X =$	1.36782
then	$100*X =$	136.782
and	$INT(100*X) =$	136
so	$INT(100*X)/100 =$	1.36

To change a batting average to three decimal places we can use a similar trick:

if	$A =$	.367891
then	$1000*A =$	367.891
and	$INT(1000*A) =$	367
so	$INT(1000*A)/1000 =$	.367

One more thing. To round this answer "up" in the third decimal place, use INT (1000*A + .5) / 1000 = .368

SELF-TEST

1. Modify and test run the BATTING AVERAGE and UNIT PRICE programs using the above techniques to appropriately change the number of decimal places in the output.

Meanwhile, back at the Casino

RND

One feature no computer language should be without is a random number generator. This is a built-in routine that produces a "surprise" number each time it's used. When a statement like

10 LET X = RND(0), or on some machines 10 LET X = RND(1)

is executed, a number between 0 and 1 is produced "randomly", and stored in X. Here's a simple test program you can use to see what these numbers look like in your BASIC.

RND DEMO

```
LIST

10 PRINT "RANDOM NOS. WITH VARIOUS MULTIPLIERS"
20 FOR K = 1 TO 10
30 LET X = RND(0)
40 PRINT X, 10*X, 100*X, INT(100*X)
50 NEXT K
60 END


RUN

RANDOM NOS. WITH VARIOUS MULTIPLIERS
 .771027        7.71027        77.1027        77
 .78183         7.8183         78.183         78
 .75174         7.5174         75.174         75
 .473969        4.73969        47.3969        47
 .781555E-1     .781555        7.81555         7
 .203217        2.03217        20.3217        20
 .5159          5.159          51.59          51
 .266449        2.66449        26.6449        26
 .955597        9.55597        95.5597        95
 .335541        3.35541        33.5541        33
```

THIS STRANGE NUMBER IS .0781555 IN DISGUISE

NOTE: Your version of BASIC will probably produce a different sequence of random numbers, but the general idea is the same. Also, RND(0) may have to be changed to RND(1) in some BASIC's. (In standard BASIC the argument—the number in parenthesis—is ignored, but in other versions it's got to be as specified in the user manual.)

Each time RND is used in line 30, a small sub-program in BASIC is used to generate a new number from the previous one. So strictly speaking, the RND numbers are "deterministic" (because they are *determined* by known formulas). In practice, however, these formulas produce numbers between 0 and 1 that don't seem to follow any predictable pattern. So they are often called "pseudo-random numbers uniformly distributed between 0 and 1."

Constants in BASIC

The numbers used in BASIC programs are called constants. So far we have used,

(1) *Integer* constants like -3, 4, 27893, and
(2) *Floating point* (or real) constants like .0831, 3.1416, and -896.28.

Another way to write a floating point constant is shown in the first column of the preceding test program where the number .781555E-1 appears.

This is called the "exponential" or "scientific" notation for writing constants. What .781555E-1 really means is

$$.781555 * 10^{-1}$$

But 10^{-1} means $1/10^1$ (remember, $10^1 = 10$), so this number is really

$(.781555) * (1/10) = .0781555$. Similarly,

$.781555E-2 = .781555 * 10^{-2} = .00781555$, and
$.781555E-3 = .781555 * 10^{-3} = .000781555$, and so on.

SIMPLE RULE #1   E-3 means "move the decimal point 3 places to the *left*."

$.781555E-3 = .000781555$

Scientific notation is used to save space when representing very small and very large numbers. (You can see that .781555E-10 takes less room to print than .0000000000781555.)

A similar notation is used to represent large numbers. For example,

$.8965E+1$ means $.8965 * 10^1 = .8965 * 10 = 8.965$
$.8965E+2$ means $.8965 * 10^2 = .8965 * 100 = 89.65$,
$.8965E+3$ means $.8965 * 10^3 = .8965 * 1000 = 896.5$,

and so on. Here, the space saving shows up for very large numbers. For example,

.8965E+18 = 896500000000000000.

SIMPLE RULE #2   E+18 means "move the decimal point 18 places to the *right*".

Simulated Craps

Now let's get back to the use of RND by writing a program to play craps. The usual rules for this dice game can be summarized in flowchart form as follows:

CRAPS FLOW CHART

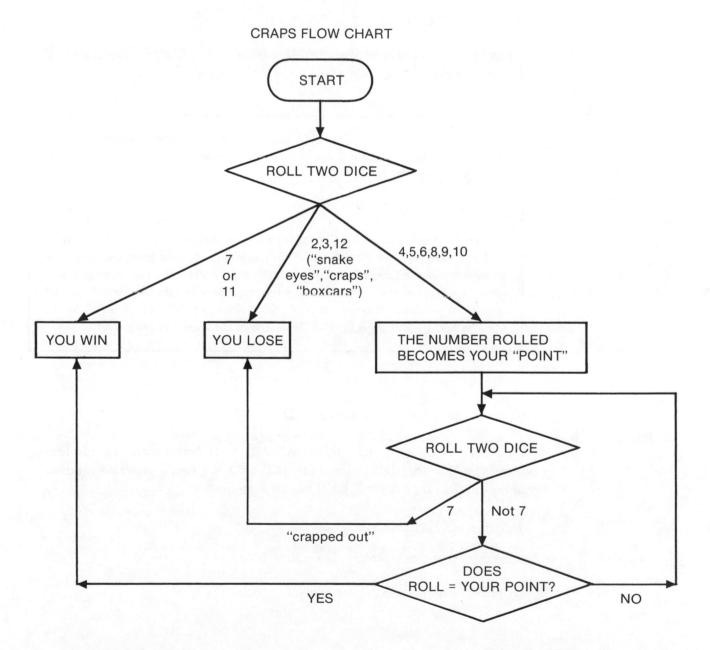

To write a program that simulates playing this game, we'll need two statements that simulate the roll of two dice by producing random integers from 1 to 6. The statements

```
30 LET D1 = INT(6*RND(0) + 1)
40 LET D2 = INT(6*RND(0) + 1)
```

do this because RND(0) produces numbers from 0 (zero) up to (but not including) 1. So for six decimal places we'd have:

		Lower Value		Upper Value
RND(0)	produces	.0000000	to	.999999
6*RND(0)	produces	.000000	to	5.999994
6*RND(0)+1	produces	1.000000	to	6.999994
INT(6*RND(0)+1)	produces	1	to	6

Thus both D1 and D2 produce integers from 1 to 6. Mathematicians say this by writing that $1 <= D1 <= 6$ and $1 <= D2 <= 6$.

Note for Statistics Buffs: Tossing 2 dice with six sides gives numbers with a total value from 2 to 12. But you will *not* get the same effect by using a "super die" with 11 sides as follows:

```
10 LET D = INT(11*RND(0) +2)
```

It's true that this statement will produce random integers from 2 to 12, but they will not show up with the same distribution you get from adding the results of tossing two 6-sided dice. For example, with one "super die", the number 7 will show up 1/11 of the time. But with two regular dice, the number 7 can be formed in six different ways, each of which shows up 1/36 of the time. So on the average, a 7 will show up 6*(1/36) = 1/6 of the time, not 1/11.

General Formula for Transforming RND

As just shown, the formula INT(6*RND(0) + 1) transforms the random numbers so that they fall in the interval $1 <= X <= 6$. To generate random numbers in the range $A <= X <= B$ use the formula

INT((B-A+1) * RND(0) +A)

Examples: To generate integers from 50 to 85 use:

```
20 LET X = INT(36*RND(0) + 50)
```

To generate two-place decimals from .50 to .85 use:

20 LET X = INT(36*RND(0) + 50)/100

To generate integers from -90 to +80 use:

20 LET X = INT(171*RND(0) - 90)

Returning to the CRAPS program, here's a listing followed by a sample run:

CRAPS
SIMULATION

```
LIST

5 RANDOMIZE
10 PRINT "SIMULATED CRAPS GAME--YOU START WITH $10"
20 LET D = 10                          ← D WILL KEEP TRACK
30 PRINT "HOW MUCH DO YOU WANT TO BET";    OF DOLLARS YOU HAVE.
40 INPUT B
50 LET D1 = INT(6*RND(0) + 1)          FIRST ROLL OF DICE.
60 LET D2 = INT(6*RND(0) + 1)
70 LET R1 = D1 + D2 ←
75 PRINT "ROLL IS";R1
80 IF R1=7 THEN 200                    REMINDER: FOR MANY MACHINES (E.G., THE
90 IF R1 = 11 THEN 200                 APPLE II) RND(0) SHOULD BE CHANGED TO RND(1).
100 IF R1 = 2 THEN 170
110 IF R1 = 3 THEN 170
120 IF R1 = 12 THEN 170                NEXT ROLL OF DICE.
130 PRINT "YOUR POINT IS";R1
140 LET R2 = INT(6*RND(0) + 1) + INT(6*RND(0) + 1) ←
145 PRINT "NEXT ROLL IS";R2
147 IF R2=7 THEN 170                   YOU LOST, SO YOUR
150 IF R2 = R1 THEN 200                BET IS SUBTRACTED
160 GOTO 140                           FROM D.
170 LET D = D - B ←
180 PRINT "TOUGH--YOU LOSE.  YOU NOW HAVE $";D
190 GOTO 220
200 LET D = D + B ←                    YOU WON, SO YOUR
210 PRINT "YOU WIN!  YOU NOW HAVE $";D  BET IS ADDED TO D.
220 PRINT "WANT TO PLAY AGAIN (1=YES)";
230 INPUT A
240 IF A = 1 THEN 30
250 PRINT "YOU ENDED WITH $";D;
260 IF D>10 THEN 290
270 PRINT "WON'T YOU EVER LEARN?"
280 STOP
290 PRINT "TALK ABOUT LUCK!"
300 END
```

This version of the program has been written to make each statement as simple as possible. Questions 5 and 6 of the Self-Test section coming up make some suggestions for shortening the program. Here's a run of the craps program. Your program may give different dice rolls because it has a different random number generator.

```
    RUN

    SIMULATED CRAPS GAME--YOU START WITH $10
    HOW MUCH DO YOU WANT TO BET? 2
    ROLL IS 10
    YOUR POINT IS 10
    NEXT ROLL IS 8
    NEXT ROLL IS 3
    NEXT ROLL IS 6
    NEXT ROLL IS 9
    NEXT ROLL IS 6
    NEXT ROLL IS 2
    NEXT ROLL IS 7
    TOUGH--YOU LOSE.  YOU NOW HAVE $ 8
    WANT TO PLAY AGAIN (1=YES)? 1
    HOW MUCH DO YOU WANT TO BET? 4
    ROLL IS 8
    YOUR POINT IS 8
    NEXT ROLL IS 5
    NEXT ROLL IS 7
    TOUGH--YOU LOSE.  YOU NOW HAVE $ 4
    WANT TO PLAY AGAIN (1=YES)? 1
    HOW MUCH DO YOU WANT TO BET? 8
    ROLL IS 3
    TOUGH--YOU LOSE.  YOU NOW HAVE $-4
    WANT TO PLAY AGAIN (1=YES)? 0
    YOU ENDED WITH $-4 WON'T YOU EVER LEARN?
    STOP at line 280
```

RANDOMIZE

If you run the craps simulation program several times, you may find that the rolls of the dice are the same for each run. This is because RND(0) always starts with the same "seed" value, and produces each new number with the same algorithm. This repeatability is very helpful for debugging programs.

To make the numbers really surprise you, there is a feature in most versions of BASIC that creates a new seed number for each run. All you have to do to get this feature is to start your program with the statement

5 RANDOMIZE   or   5 RANDOM

To see what happens, run the craps program twice with RANDOMIZE, and twice without.

> NOTE: Some versions of BASIC don't have a RANDOMIZE. Their normal way of operating is to give you a different sequence of random numbers on each run. For these systems, if you want the same sequence of random numbers on each run, you must put a statement like 5 Z=RND (-1) at the beginning of the program.

ON...GOTO...

This is sometimes called the "computed GOTO" statement. It branches to different line numbers, depending on the value of a variable placed right after the word ON. Here's a program that demonstrates how it works:

QUIZ

```
LIST

10  PRINT "QUIZ:  WHO WAS THE 4TH MARX BROTHER?"
20  PRINT "1 = ZIPPO, 2 = HARRY, 3 = ZEPPO"
30  INPUT A
40  ON A GO TO 50, 70, 90
50  PRINT "NO, YOU'RE THINKING OF A CIGAR LIGHTER--TRY AGAIN."
60  GOTO 30
70  PRINT "YOU MAY BE WILD ABOUT HARRY, BUT THAT'S NOT RIGHT."
71  PRINT "TRY AGAIN."
80  GOTO 30
90  PRINT "BY GEORGE YOU'VE GOT IT!!"
100 END

Ready

RUN

QUIZ:  WHO WAS THE 4TH MARX BROTHER?
1 = ZIPPO, 2 = HARRY, 3 = ZEPPO
? 2
YOU MAY BE WILD ABOUT HARRY, BUT THAT'S NOT RIGHT.
TRY AGAIN.
? 1
NO, YOU'RE THINKING OF A CIGAR LIGHTER--TRY AGAIN.
? 3
BY GEORGE YOU'VE GOT IT!!
```

> IF A=1, GO TO 50
> IF A=2, GO TO 70
> IF A=3, GO TO 90

Here's a program that uses RND with ON...GOTO... to generate random messages. If you analyze the output, you can see that RND must have produced the integers 4, 4, 4, 2, 1, 1, 3, 2, 4, 2 which caused branches to lines 100, 100, 100, 60, 40, 40, 80, 60, 100, 60.

HICCUP

```
LIST

5  RANDOMIZE
10 FOR N=1 TO 10
20 LET K=INT (4*RND(0)+1)
30 ON K GO TO 40, 60, 80, 100
40 PRINT "HEE-";
50 GO TO 110
60 PRINT "HA-";
70 GO TO 110
80 PRINT "HIC-";
90 GO TO 110
100 PRINT "HO-";
110 NEXT N
120 END


RUN

HO-HO-HO-HA-HEE-HEE-HIC-HA-HO-HA-
```

SELF-TEST

1. Simulate running the following program, using a die to produce the random numbers in line 80. What application do you see for this program?

```
10 LET K1 = 0
20 LET K2 = 0
30 LET K3 = 0
40 LET K4 = 0
50 LET K5 = 0
60 LET K6 = 0
70 FOR N = 1 TO 600
80 LET R = INT(6*RND(0) + 1)
90 ON R GO TO 140, 150, 160, 170, 180, 190
140 LET K1 = K1 + 1
145 GO TO 210
150 LET K2 = K2 + 1
155 GO TO 210
160 LET K3 = K3 + 1
165 GO TO 210
170 LET K4 = K4 + 1
175 GO TO 210
180 LET K5 = K5 + 1
185 GO TO 210
190 LET K6 = K6 + 1
210 NEXT N
230 PRINT K1; K2; K3; K4; K5; K6
240 END
```

2. You didn't really do #1 completely did you? Six hundred die tosses is a bit much. To get some real insight about RND from this program, you should run it on your computer.

3. Play the CRAPS program using the strategy of doubling your bet each time. Will this always guarantee that you eventually come out ahead? What feature can be added to the program to make this strategy less threatening to the "house"?

4. Modify the CRAPS program so a FOR...NEXT loop controls how often it plays. Then run it for a large number of plays (say 100, 200, 300, etc.) printing only the final value of D. The program itself should make the bets, using various strategies (e.g., always bet $1, for example). See what you can discover about the odds of winning this game for various strategies.

5. Can you find five statements in the CRAPS program that can be replaced with a single statement? Hint, try:

80 ON R1 GOTO 130, 170, 170, 130, 130, 130, 200, 130, 130, 130, 200, 170

6. Can you replace statements 50, 60, 70, and 75 in the CRAPS program with a single statement?

2.7   HOUR 7: PROGRAMS TO HELP MOM AND DAD PASS ARITHMETIC 102

Very few people who have "taken" a foreign language in school are fluent in its use. Little children from countries where that language is spoken do a lot better, and with far less fuss. The same is true of the "languages" of mathematics and science. Achieving fluency in their use is much easier in settings where they are spoken regularly.

Personal computers make it possible to create such settings in some very interesting ways. One of the best involves computer game programs, and there's an entire chapter on games coming up. In this section we'll help prepare the way by explaining some of the techniques used in writing number-oriented games.

ABS

ABS(X) is a function which "processes" X in a very simple manner. It merely changes the sign of X to +. This is useful when we want to check how close some INPUT data supplied by the user comes to another value (say, the one the program expects). The ABS (absolute value) function helps by giving the "distance" between the two numbers . For example,

    ABS(8 - 5) = 3
    ABS(5 - 8) = 3
    ABS(5 - 2) = 3
    ABS(2 - 5) = 3

As you can see, ABS tells us that in all of these cases, the distance between the numbers is 3. Here's an example using this feature:

NUMBER GUESS

```
LIST

3 RANDOMIZE
5 FOR K=1 TO 3
10 LET R = INT(10 * RND(0) + 1)
20 PRINT "PICK A NUMBER FROM 1 TO 10";
30 INPUT N
40 IF R = N THEN 110
50 PRINT "NO, YOU MISSED BY";ABS(N - R)
60 PRINT "TRY ONE MORE TIME.  NUMBER IS";
70 INPUT N
80 IF R = N THEN 110
90 PRINT "YOU BLEW IT.  THE NUMBER WAS";R
100 GOTO 120
110 PRINT "RIGHT!!!"
120 NEXT K
130 END


RUN

PICK A NUMBER FROM 1 TO 10? 5
NO, YOU MISSED BY 3
TRY ONE MORE TIME.  NUMBER IS? 8
RIGHT!!!
PICK A NUMBER FROM 1 TO 10? 1
NO, YOU MISSED BY 7
TRY ONE MORE TIME.  NUMBER IS? 8
RIGHT!!!
PICK A NUMBER FROM 1 TO 10? 10
NO, YOU MISSED BY 2
TRY ONE MORE TIME.  NUMBER IS? 8
RIGHT!!!
```

THIS IS THE COMPUTER'S NUMBER

THIS IS YOUR NUMBER.

THIS GIVES THE AMOUNT BY WHICH N MISSED, BUT NOT THE SIGN.

WITH THESE CHOICES YOU CAN ALWAYS GET IT ON THE 2ND CHANCE.

Another use of ABS is for accepting input that is "close enough" even though not exactly the number expected. The art of getting such "ball park" estimates is seldom taught in school, yet it's a valuable one. Here's an example of a program for practicing this:

APPROXIMATE
ARITHMETIC

```
LIST

3 RANDOMIZE
5 FOR K = 1 TO 10
10 LET H = INT(4000 * RND(0) + 1200)/100
20 LET M = INT(1000 * RND(0) + 500)/100
30 LET I = INT(300 * RND(0) + 300)/100
40 LET D = INT(9 * RND(0) + 1)
50 PRINT "APPROXIMATELY HOW MUCH SHOULD YOU BUDGET"
55 PRINT "FOR A TRIP OF";D;"DAYS IF--"
60 PRINT "   HOTEL COST PER DAY   = $";H
70 PRINT "   MEAL COST PER DAY    = $";M
80 PRINT "   INCIDENTALS PER DAY  = $";I
90 INPUT A
100 LET C = D * (H + M + I)
110 LET E = ABS(A - C)
120 IF E/C < .10 THEN 160
130 PRINT "YOU MISSED BY $";E
140 PRINT "YOU WERE OFF BY";(E/C)*100;"%"
150 GOTO 180
160 PRINT "VERY GOOD.  YOU WERE OFF BY $";E
170 PRINT "THAT WAS AN ERROR OF ONLY";(E/C)*100;"%"
180 NEXT K
190 END
```

```
RUN

APPROXIMATELY HOW MUCH SHOULD YOU BUDGET
FOR A TRIP OF 5 DAYS IF--
   HOTEL COST PER DAY   = $ 42.84
   MEAL COST PER DAY    = $ 12.81
   INCIDENTALS PER DAY = $ 5.25
? 60
YOU MISSED BY $ 244.5
YOU WERE OFF BY 80.2956 %
APPROXIMATELY HOW MUCH SHOULD YOU BUDGET
FOR A TRIP OF 3 DAYS IF--
   HOTEL COST PER DAY   = $ 15.12
   MEAL COST PER DAY    = $ 7.03
   INCIDENTALS PER DAY = $ 4.54
? 76
VERY GOOD.  YOU WERE OFF BY $ 4.07
THAT WAS AN ERROR OF ONLY 5.08305 %
APPROXIMATELY HOW MUCH SHOULD YOU BUDGET
FOR A TRIP OF 5 DAYS IF--
   HOTEL COST PER DAY   = $ 50.22
   MEAL COST PER DAY    = $ 8.35
   INCIDENTALS PER DAY = $ 4.23
? 320
VERY GOOD.  YOU WERE OFF BY $ 6
THAT WAS AN ERROR OF ONLY 1.91083 %
APPROXIMATELY HOW MUCH SHOULD YOU BUDGET
FOR A TR^C
```

THIS SHOULD HAVE BEEN DONE MENTALLY USING $43 + 13 + 5 = 61 \times 5 = 305$.

Notice that we used two kinds of "error" formulas in this program. The absolute error E = ABS(A - C) gives the absolute value of the *difference* between the correct answer and the approximate answer, while the relative error E/C shows the *ratio* between this difference and the correct answer.

Why make this distinction? Well suppose you were a contractor who made a bid that missed the true cost by $1000. How serious is this? It all depends. If you take two extreme cases, you'll see why.

Case 1:
True cost = $50,000
Your bid   = $49,000
Absolute error = $1,000
Relative error = 1000/50000 = .02
percent error = 2%

Case 2:
True cost = $2,500
Your bid   = $1,500
Absolute error = $1,000
Relative error = 1000/2500 = .4
Percent error = 40%

The absolute error was the same in both cases. It's the relative error that shows which one is a disaster. (Percent error also shows this since it is merely relative error multiplied by 100.)

ABS is also handy in making sure that an input response is as requested. Here's one way this can be done:

INPUT CHECK

```
LIST

10  PRINT "TYPE A POSITIVE INTEGER BETWEEN 50 AND 100."
20  INPUT A
30  IF INT(A) <> A THEN 120
40  IF ABS(75-A) > 25 THEN 140
50  PRINT "YOU HAVE OBEYED A COMPUTER."
60  PRINT "THERE IS NO HOPE."
70  STOP
120 PRINT "THAT'S NOT AN INTEGER."
130 GO TO 10
140 PRINT "OUT OF REQUESTED RANGE."
145 PRINT "READ THE INSTRUCTIONS CAREFULLY."
150 GO TO 10
160 END



RUN

TYPE A POSITIVE INTEGER BETWEEN 50 AND 100.
? 25
OUT OF REQUESTED RANGE.
READ THE INSTRUCTIONS CAREFULLY.
TYPE A POSITIVE INTEGER BETWEEN 50 AND 100.
? 7.5
THAT'S NOT AN INTEGER.
TYPE A POSITIVE INTEGER BETWEEN 50 AND 100.
? 75
YOU HAVE OBEYED A COMPUTER.
THERE IS NO HOPE.
STOP at line 70
```

If you want to be more explicit in your error messages, statement 40 can be replaced by two tests:

```
40 IF A < 50 THEN 140
45 IF A > 100 THEN 142

    .
    .

    .
140 PRINT "TOO SMALL!"
141 GO TO 145
142 PRINT "TOO LARGE!"
    .
    .
    .
```

SQR

We'll finish this section with a math game program that uses the square root function of BASIC . SQR(X) processes the number X by finding its square root and "returning" this value in the place where SQR is used. (The square root of X is a number which when multiplied by itself gives X. This means you must use positive numbers for X. Otherwise you'll get an error message.)

Example:

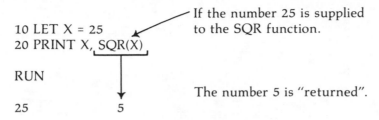

10 LET X = 25
20 PRINT X, SQR(X)

RUN

25   5

If the number 25 is supplied
to the SQR function.

The number 5 is "returned".

Here's a game program to practice estimating square roots:

SQUARE ROOT
QUIZ

```
LIST

5 RANDOMIZE
10 LET K = 0
20 PRINT "TO WIN THE GOLD STAR YOU NEED 3 ANSWERS IN A ROW"
25 PRINT "THAT HAVE LESS THAN 5% ERROR."
30 PRINT "----------------------------------------------------"
50 LET R = INT(100*RND(0) + 1)
60 PRINT "WHAT IS THE SQUARE ROOT OF";R
70 INPUT A
80 LET C = SQR(R)
90 IF ABS(A - C)/C < .05 THEN 130
100 PRINT "NOT TOO CLOSE.  SQUARE ROOT OF ";R;"IS";C
105 PRINT "YOU MISSED BY";100*ABS(A/C-1);"%"
106 PRINT
110 LET K = 0
120 GO TO 50
130 PRINT "NOT BAD--YOU ONLY MISSED BY";100*ABS(A/C-1);"%"
135 PRINT "SQUARE ROOT OF ";R;"IS";C
136 PRINT
140 LET K = K + 1
150 IF K < 3 THEN 50
160 PRINT "THAT'S 3 IN A ROW!      *****"
170 PRINT "   PASTE STAR HERE--     *   *"
175 PRINT "                        *****"
180 END
```

```
RUN

TO WIN THE GOLD STAR YOU NEED 3 ANSWERS IN A ROW
THAT HAVE LESS THAN 5% ERROR.
----------------------------------------------------
WHAT IS THE SQUARE ROOT OF 78
? 8.11
NOT TOO CLOSE.  SQUARE ROOT OF  78 IS 8.83176
YOU MISSED BY 8.17233 %

WHAT IS THE SQUARE ROOT OF 79
? 8.8
NOT BAD--YOU ONLY MISSED BY .992265 %
SQUARE ROOT OF  79 IS 8.88819
```

```
        WHAT IS THE SQUARE ROOT OF 76
        ? 8.5
        NOT BAD--YOU ONLY MISSED BY 2.49831 %
        SQUARE ROOT OF  76 IS 8.7178

        WHAT IS THE SQUARE ROOT OF 48
        ? 6.10
        NOT TOO CLOSE.  SQUARE ROOT OF  48 IS 6.9282
        YOU MISSED BY 11.9541 %

        WHAT IS THE SQUARE ROOT OF 8
        ? 6.4
        NOT TOO CLOSE.  SQUARE ROOT OF  8 IS 2.82843
        YOU MISSED BY 126.274 %

        WHAT IS THE SQUARE ROOT OF 21
        ? 4.68
        NOT BAD--YOU ONLY MISSED BY 2.12597 %
        SQUARE ROOT OF  21 IS 4.58258

        WHAT IS THE SQUARE ROOT OF 52
        ? 7.57
        NOT BAD--YOU ONLY MISSED BY 4.97701 %
        SQUARE ROOT OF  52 IS 7.2111

        WHAT IS THE SQUARE ROOT OF 27
        ? 5.15
        NOT BAD--YOU ONLY MISSED BY .888204 %
        SQUARE ROOT OF  27 IS 5.19615

        THAT'S 3 IN A ROW!    *****
          PASTE STAR HERE--    *   *
                              *****
```

Notice that the user had to supply an answer within 5% three times in a row before getting the "gold star".

For a really fiendish game, make the 5% a variable that gets smaller each time. Start with V=.05, and then make V=.7*V each time around.

REM

We have been explaining programs by drawing "balloons" on the side which contain explanatory remarks. Remarks can also be placed within a program by use of the REM statement which looks like this:

10 REM ANYTHING YOU WANT TO SAY

Remark statements only show up when you list a program, *not* during a run. Here's an example of how one of our previous programs might look with REM statements. It also illustrates a feature in *some* BASIC's which allows remarks after the ! or ' symbol.

REMARK
DEMO

```
LIST

10  REM---PROGRAM FOR CHECKING INPUT---------------
15  PRINT "TYPE A POSITIVE INTEGER BETWEEN 50 AND 100"
20  INPUT A
25  REM---FIRST SEE IF MAYBE IT'S NOT AN INTEGER---
30  IF INT(A) <> A THEN 120
35  REM---NOW SEE IF IT'S OUTSIDE RANGE 50 TO 100---
40  IF ABS(75-A) > 25 THEN 140
50  PRINT "YOU HAVE OBEYED A COMPUTER."
60  PRINT "THERE IS NO HOPE."
70  STOP
115 REM---MESSAGE FOR LINE 30 BRANCH---          !
120 PRINT "THAT'S NOT AN INTEGER"                ! THIS IS THE
130 GOTO 10                                      ! SECTION OF
135 REM---MESSAGE FOR LINE 35 BRANCH---          ! THE PROGRAM
140 PRINT "OUT OF REQUESTED RANGE"               ! THAT PRINTS
145 PRINT "READ THE INSTRUCTIONS CAREFULLY"      ! MESSAGES
150 GOTO 10                                      !
160 END
```

SELF-TEST

1. Simulate a RUN of this program:

```
10 FOR K = 1 TO 10
20 LET X = K * K
30 PRINT K, SQR(X)
40 NEXT K
50 END
```

2. Simulate a RUN of this "pattern" program:

```
10 FOR K = 10 TO -10 STEP -1
20 FOR J = 1 TO ABS(K)
30 PRINT "*";
40 NEXT J
50 PRINT
60 NEXT K
70 END
```

3. Write, debug, and run a program that asks for an estimate of the total cost of 5 items on a supermarket receipt. First have the computer print out the simulated receipt. Generate the dollar cost of each item with INT(900*RND(0) + 20) / 100). Then ask for an estimated total, and compare it with the exact sum. Give different kinds of congratulatory (or other) messages that depend on the relative error in each answer.

2.8   HOUR 8: KEEPING CHECK ON A BANK BALANCE

In this section we'll explain two new features of BASIC (subroutines and user-defined functions) by showing how to apply them to the problem of calculating compound interest. Before discussing these features, let's first review what's involved in finding interest that's "compounded" at various intervals.

The idea of compounding shows up in several kinds of problems. For example, in calculating the population growth of some species (say rabbits), you have to allow for the fact that if new rabbits come from the original population, then new, new rabbits come from both the new rabbits and the original population, while new, new, new rabbits come from the new, new rabbits, new rabbits, and original rabbits (assuming no deaths), etc., etc.

The same idea holds for compound interest: it's calculated on the original amount (called the principal), and on the interest on the principal, and on the interest on the interest on the principal, etc., etc. How often this re-calculation gets done is up to the bank. For example, they may do it four times a year (which is called quarterly compounding), or even 365 times a year (called daily compounding). There are two methods for calculating compound interest: (1) use a loop, and (2) use an exponential formula. Let's look at the loop method first.

Here's a loop for finding 5% interest compounded quarterly on a principal of $1000, with a total time in the bank of 1 year.

```
 5 LET N = 1000
10 FOR K = 1 TO 4
20 LET N = N + (.05/4) * N
30 NEXT K
40 PRINT "INTEREST IS"; N - 1000
```

The new balance at the end of each quarter (3 months) is calculated in line 20 as follows.

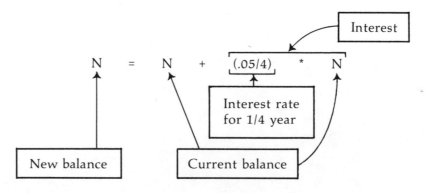

Each time around the FOR...NEXT loop is like another 3 months. At the end of 4 loops, N contains the year-end balance, so N - 1000 gives the compound interest that accumulated in a year.

To do this same calculation for daily compounding, the loop would have to go FOR K = 1 TO 365, while the interest added each day would be at the rate of (.05/365).

GOSUB

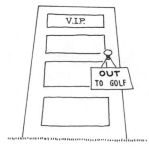

The small program we just explained can be used as part of a larger (or "main") program. The small program can be called a "subprogram", or a "subroutine".

The advantage to building a main program partially from subroutines is that it helps organize your thinking. The approach to take is to think of yourself as the VIP (very important programmer). You start by pretending that you don't have to worry about details because you can call on assistants for help. To make the idea even more dramatic, you can picture your executive office on the top floor, while the assistants work at lower levels called subroutines. When you need help from an assistant (say at level 1000) you shout "GOSUB 1000". When the assistant at this location is finished, he yells "RETURN". This image isn't as silly as it may seem. To see why, let's first look at a "program" written by a VIP which only outlines the work to be done.

10 Get data on husband's bank account.

    ⋮

50 Get my assistant down on level 1000 to figure out and
    print husband's interest and balance.

    ⋮

65 Get data on wife's bank account.

    ⋮

90 Ask the same assistant to figure out wife's interest and
    balance, and print it.
100 Lock up office and go play golf.

If written in BASIC, such a program would partially look like the following:

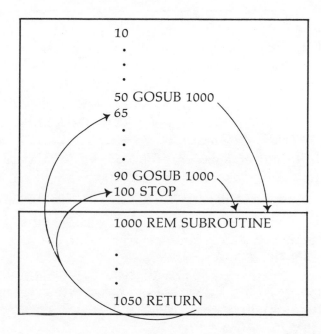

What the statement GOSUB 1000 really means is "go and do the subroutine that starts at line 1000 and then return to the line right after the GOSUB statement that was just executed". To see how this all goes together, look at the following complete program:

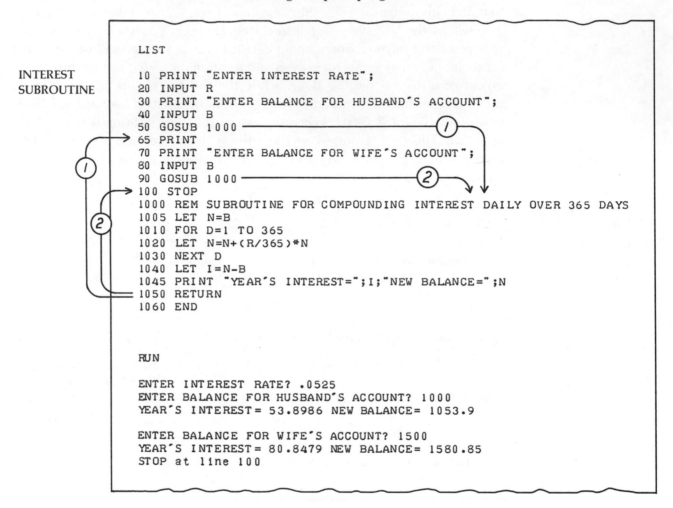

INTEREST
SUBROUTINE

```
LIST

10  PRINT "ENTER INTEREST RATE";
20  INPUT R
30  PRINT "ENTER BALANCE FOR HUSBAND'S ACCOUNT";
40  INPUT B
50  GOSUB 1000
65  PRINT
70  PRINT "ENTER BALANCE FOR WIFE'S ACCOUNT";
80  INPUT B
90  GOSUB 1000
100 STOP
1000 REM SUBROUTINE FOR COMPOUNDING INTEREST DAILY OVER 365 DAYS
1005 LET N=B
1010 FOR D=1 TO 365
1020 LET N=N+(R/365)*N
1030 NEXT D
1040 LET I=N-B
1045 PRINT "YEAR'S INTEREST=";I;"NEW BALANCE=";N
1050 RETURN
1060 END


RUN

ENTER INTEREST RATE? .0525
ENTER BALANCE FOR HUSBAND'S ACCOUNT? 1000
YEAR'S INTEREST= 53.8986 NEW BALANCE= 1053.9

ENTER BALANCE FOR WIFE'S ACCOUNT? 1500
YEAR'S INTEREST= 80.8479 NEW BALANCE= 1580.85
STOP at line 100
```

All the hard work is done in the subroutine from lines 1000 to 1050. When the main program reaches line 50, it "goes to" line 1000, where it continues execution. In our example, it does line 1005, followed by 365 times around the FOR...NEXT loop in 1010 to 1030, followed by 1040, followed by 1045 and 1050. Line 1050 then says RETURN. (Subroutines must always end with a RETURN statement.) Return means go back to the line *right after* the GOSUB. In our example, that's line 65. So 65 is executed right after 1050. The second time the subroutine is called is at line 90. Again all the hard work is done in the subroutine (at no extra cost in programming!), but this time the RETURN is to line 100.

Details, Details

Now that we see the big picture, we can concentrate on explaining how this particular subroutine works. What it does is to start the new balance out as

N = B, calculate the interest for one day as (.0525/365)*N, and then get the revised new balance as N = N + (.0525/365)*N. This process is repeated 365 times in a loop. When the loop is finished, the interest earned for a year will be the final new balance minus the starting balance, that is, I = N - B. Now that we have N and I, we can return to line 65, where the program continues. When the program gets to line 90, this whole process is repeated, but this time B contains the wife's balance, so a completely different calculation is done. In other words, *subroutines in BASIC use the current value that variables have in the main program* .

Question: Could this program have been written as easily using GOTO instead of GOSUB? No, because there would be no way to return to different line numbers the way RETURN does.

Question: Can subroutines sometimes be inefficient? The answer is yes, but after everything is working, you can swap your VIP hat for your STP hat (super terrific programmer), and clean things up a bit. For example, the subroutine we have shown does the division (R/365) seven hundred and thirty times! This inefficiency can be removed by adding the statement

25 LET F = R/365

and using F instead of R/365 inside the subroutine.

DEF FNX

As just seen, subroutines are small programs, usually involving several lines. Sometimes a "subjob" can be handled by a single LET statement, and using a subroutine is hardly worth the effort. In this case, there's another feature called DEFining a function that can be used instead of GOSUB. We'll illustrate its use with the second method for calculating compound interest.

If you dig through some math books, you'll find the following formula for getting the new balance on an account with compound interest:

$$N = P * (1 + R/M)\uparrow(M * T)$$

In this formula,
    P is the starting principal in dollars,
    R is the annual interest rate,
    M is the number of times interest is compounded each year, and
    T is the number of years left in the bank.

For example, for $3000 left for three years in a bank with 5% interest compounded monthly,

P = 3000
R = .05
M = 12
T = 3

So the new amount at the end of three years is

$$N = 3000 * (1 + .05/12)\uparrow(12 * 3).$$

The 'up arrow' means raise to that power (exponentiate), so this is a difficult calculation. It's time for a computer!

Our programming approach will be to place this formula in a special statement that allows the formula to be called upon as often as we wish. The way to "store" a formula like this in a BASIC program is to use the define function statement as follows:

$$10 \ \underline{\text{DEF FNN}} \ \underline{(P, R, M, T)} = \underline{P * (1 + R/M) \uparrow (M * T)}$$

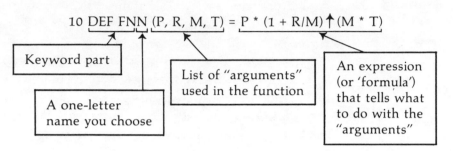

Keyword part

A one-letter name you choose

List of "arguments" used in the function

An expression (or 'formula') that tells what to do with the "arguments"

The DEF FNN statement can be placed anywhere in a program, and FNN can be used anywhere that an expression can be used. Here's a program that uses our function twice, once in a LET statement, once in a PRINT statement. We called our function FNN. We could just as well have used names like FNA, FNB, FNC, ..., FNZ.

INTEREST FUNCTION

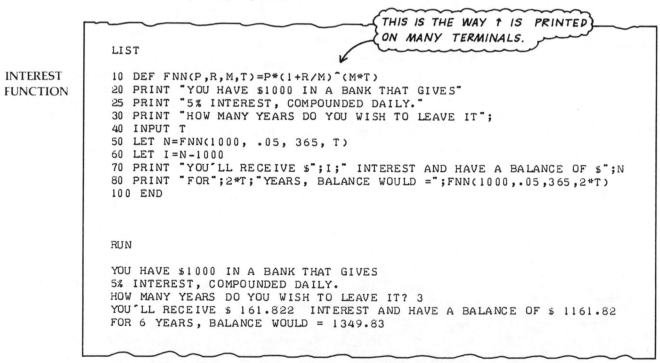

> THIS IS THE WAY ↑ IS PRINTED ON MANY TERMINALS.

```
LIST

10  DEF FNN(P,R,M,T)=P*(1+R/M)^(M*T)
20  PRINT "YOU HAVE $1000 IN A BANK THAT GIVES"
25  PRINT "5% INTEREST, COMPOUNDED DAILY."
30  PRINT "HOW MANY YEARS DO YOU WISH TO LEAVE IT";
40  INPUT T
50  LET N=FNN(1000, .05, 365, T)
60  LET I=N-1000
70  PRINT "YOU'LL RECEIVE $";I;" INTEREST AND HAVE A BALANCE OF $";N
80  PRINT "FOR";2*T;"YEARS, BALANCE WOULD =";FNN(1000,.05,365,2*T)
100 END



RUN

YOU HAVE $1000 IN A BANK THAT GIVES
5% INTEREST, COMPOUNDED DAILY.
HOW MANY YEARS DO YOU WISH TO LEAVE IT? 3
YOU'LL RECEIVE $ 161.822  INTEREST AND HAVE A BALANCE OF $ 1161.82
FOR 6 YEARS, BALANCE WOULD = 1349.83
```

As shown in lines 50 and 80, when FNN is used (or "called") it must be given arguments. Notice that these arguments can be replaced with constants, variables, or even expressions.

ON...GOSUB

This statement is similar to the ON...GOTO statement. It directs the program to go to different subroutines, depending on the value of the variable (or expression) right after the keyword ON

```
   :
   :
10 ON K GOSUB 1000, 1500, 2000
20 PRINT
   :
   :
```

means "if K = 1, go to subroutine 1000, return to line 20",
        "if K = 2, go to subroutine 1500, return to line 20",
        "if K = 3, go to subroutine 2000, return to line 20".

It's up to the programmer to make sure that K only takes on values that match the number of subroutines. If, for example, K became 4 in our example, standard BASIC would treat this as an error (some earlier versions treated this as a "default" and continued execution at the next line—line 20 in our example). For an example of ON...GOSUB, see SELF-TEST Question 3.

SELF-TEST

1. Simulate running this program:

```
10 PRINT "TYPE AN INTEGER FROM 1 TO 5"
20 INPUT I
30 IF INT(I)<>I THEN 10
40 IF ABS(I-3)>2 THEN 10
50 PRINT "HOW DO ";
55 LET N = I
60 GOSUB 500
100 PRINT
110 PRINT "OR IS IT ALREADY POSSIBLE ";
120 LET N=2 * I
130 GOSUB 500
140 STOP
500 FOR K = 1 TO N
510 PRINT "YOU KNOW ";
520 NEXT K
530 RETURN
540 END
```

2. Simulate running this program:

```
10 DEF FNA(R) = 3.1416 * R * R
20 FOR K = 1 TO 5
30 PRINT "FOR A RADIUS OF";20+K
40 PRINT "THE AREA OF A CIRCLE IS";FNA(20+K)
50 NEXT K
60 END
```

3. Write and run this program:

```
10 FOR K = 1 TO 10
20 PRINT "MAY ";
30 LET X = INT(4 * RND(0) + 1)
40 ON X GOSUB 100, 200, 300, 400
50 PRINT "SING TO ";
60 LET Y = INT (4 * RND(0) + 1)
70 ON Y GOSUB 100, 200, 300, 400
75 PRINT
80 NEXT K
90 STOP
100 PRINT "AN IMPORTED SALAMI ";
110 RETURN
200 PRINT "YOUR FAITHFUL DOG ";
210 RETURN
300 PRINT "AN ENRAGED CAMEL ";
310 RETURN
400 PRINT "THE EASTER BUNNY ";
410 RETURN
500 END
```

4. Write a program that compares the "loop" method with the "formula" method for getting compound interest. Show the results at the end of each year. A RUN should look like this:

```
PRINCIPAL? 1000
INTEREST RATE? .05
# OF TIMES COMPOUNDED PER YEAR? 365
# OF YEARS? 25
STARTING YEAR? 1976
THANK YOU
```

	LOOP METHOD		FORMULA METHOD	
YEAR	BALANCE	INTEREST	BALANCE	INTEREST
1976	1000	0	1000	0
1977	1051.27	51.2745	1051.27	51.2663
1978	1105.16	53.9032	1105.16	53.8945
1979	1161.82	56.6667	1161.82	56.6574
.	.	.	.	.
.	.	.	.	.
2001	3490.05	170.223	3489.94	170.191

Our program ignored leap years. If you're really ambitious, see if you can take leap years into account. The output of this program will vary slightly on different computers due to what are called "rounding" errors. The only way around this problem is to use a BASIC with double-precision arithmetic.

2.9   PROJECT IDEAS

1. Write a program that allows the user to enter the date of deposit, the amount deposited, the annual interest rate, the number of times compounded per year, and the date of withdrawal. The program should then print the new balance and the interest accumulated. A date like November 18, 1976 can be entered as:

   DATE DEP? 11, 18, 76

   You can ignore leap years if you wish. Another simplification is to treat all months as having 30 days, which means assuming 360 days for one year (some banking systems do this). Sub-project: How can a bank advertise that 5.5% interest compounded daily amounts to an annual interest rate of 5.73%?

2. Write an arithmetic practice program that uses four subroutines: one for addition problems, one for subtraction, one for multiplication, one for division. The RND function and ON...GOSUB should then be used to select the kind of problem (addition, subtraction, multiplication, or division) to be presented. Also try to use the method of SELF-TEST Question 3 to produce different kinds of messages for wrong answers, and other kinds of messages for correct answers. Here's what a RUN might look like:

   ADDITION QUESTION; 5 + 6 = ? 11
   RIGHT! YOUR REWARD WILL BE RICHES AND RIPE BANANAS.
   SUBTRACTION QUESTION; 33 - 23 = ? 16
   WRONG—ANSWER IS 10
   KEEP THIS UP AND YOU'LL FIND CHICKEN LIVERS IN YOUR SOCKS
   DIVISION QUESTION: ...etc. ...

3. It's legal to have one subroutine call another subroutine in BASIC. The program below illustrates this feature. Study and run the program, and then write it *without* using GOSUB at all. Your program should produce the same output as shown in our example.

SUBMARINE

```
LIST

5 RANDOMIZE
10 PRINT "PLAYER #1 TYPE RANGE (0 TO 50)";
20 INPUT P
30 LET R = 50 * RND(0)
40 LET D1 = ABS(P - R)
50 GOSUB 1000
60 PRINT "PLAYER #2 TYPE RANGE (0 TO 50)";
70 INPUT P
80 LET R = 50 * RND(0)
90 LET D2 = ABS(P-R)
100 GOSUB 1000
110 IF D1 = D2 THEN 170
120 IF D1 < D2 THEN 150
130 PRINT "PLAYER #2 WINS"
140 GOTO 180
150 PRINT "PLAYER #1 WINS"
160 GOTO 180
170 PRINT " TIE SCORE"
180 GOTO 9999
```

```
1000 REM--------TARGET DISPLAY ROUTINE-----
1010 GOSUB 2000
1020 LET X = P
1025 PRINT "SHELL";
1030 GOSUB 3000
1040 GOSUB 2000
1050 LET X = R
1055 PRINT "U-BOAT";
1060 GOSUB 3000
1070 GOSUB 2000
1080 PRINT
1090 RETURN
2000 REM--------LINE ROUTINE-----
2010 FOR K=1 TO 60
2020 PRINT "-";
2030 NEXT K
2040 PRINT
2050 RETURN
3000 REM--------SHELL ROUTINE-----
3010 PRINT TAB(X+8);"<*>"
3020 RETURN
9999 END
```

```
RUN

PLAYER #1 TYPE RANGE (0 TO 50)? 35
------------------------------------------------------------
SHELL                                            <*>
------------------------------------------------------------
U-BOAT                                             <*>
------------------------------------------------------------

PLAYER #2 TYPE RANGE (0 TO 50)? 10
------------------------------------------------------------
SHELL                  <*>
------------------------------------------------------------
U-BOAT                                             <*>
------------------------------------------------------------

PLAYER #1 WINS
```

4. Find a program written in an extended version of BASIC, and translate it into a version that runs on your system. The idea is to become familiar with the possibilities of extended BASIC so you can get a feel for those features you want to insist on in buying your next software package. It would also be a good idea to keep a notebook on the special features of your BASIC.

SOLUTION

We'll show a sample solution to this project as a guide to what's involved. Our solution will also help you to read programs written in BASIC-PLUS or EXTENDED BASIC. You'll see that most of the extensions can easily be translated into minimal standard BASIC, but at the cost of extra statements.

Our example will first show a Russian Roulette Game program written in extended BASIC. Then we'll illustrate how each of the extended statements can be replaced by several simpler statements.

BASIC-PLUS ROULETTE

```
LIST

10  RANDOMIZE
20  PRINT "RUSSIAN ROULETTE": PRINT "------------"
30  PRINT "TYPE 1 TO SPIN CHAMBER, 0 TO QUIT"
35  N=0
40  INPUT "YOUR CHOICE IS"; C
60  IF C=1 THEN PRINT "LOTSALUCK" ELSE PRINT "CHICKEN": GOTO 140
70  IF RND(1)>.85 THEN 100 ELSE N=N+1
80  IF N>=10 THEN 120 ELSE PRINT "--CLICK--"
90  PRINT: GOTO 40
100 PRINT "  BANG!!!  YOU'RE DEAD":  PRINT "SORRY ABOUT THAT"
110 PRINT: PRINT "NEXT VICTIM PLEASE":PRINT:GOTO 30
120 PRINT "YOU DID IT!!  10 MISSES! -- YOU WIN"
125 FOR K=1 TO 10: PRINT "YEA! ";: NEXT K: PRINT
130 STOP
140 PRINT "GET SOMEONE ELSE WHO ISN'T SO SMART": PRINT: GOTO 30
150 END
```

STD. BASIC ROULETTE

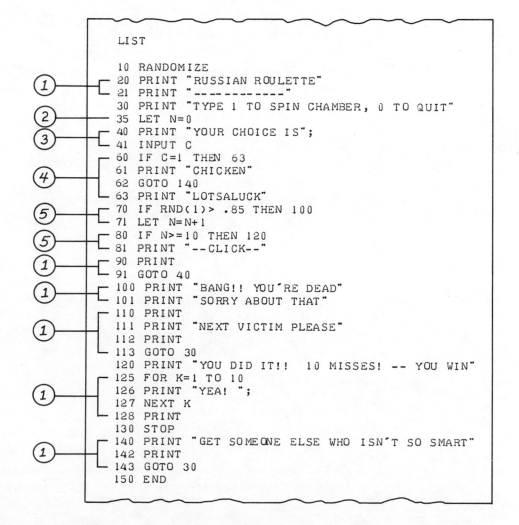

```
LIST

10  RANDOMIZE
20  PRINT "RUSSIAN ROULETTE"
21  PRINT "------------"
30  PRINT "TYPE 1 TO SPIN CHAMBER, 0 TO QUIT"
35  LET N=0
40  PRINT "YOUR CHOICE IS";
41  INPUT C
60  IF C=1 THEN 63
61  PRINT "CHICKEN"
62  GOTO 140
63  PRINT "LOTSALUCK"
70  IF RND(1)> .85 THEN 100
71  LET N=N+1
80  IF N>=10 THEN 120
81  PRINT "--CLICK--"
90  PRINT
91  GOTO 40
100 PRINT "BANG!! YOU'RE DEAD"
101 PRINT "SORRY ABOUT THAT"
110 PRINT
111 PRINT "NEXT VICTIM PLEASE"
112 PRINT
113 GOTO 30
120 PRINT "YOU DID IT!!  10 MISSES! -- YOU WIN"
125 FOR K=1 TO 10
126 PRINT "YEA! ";
127 NEXT K
128 PRINT
130 STOP
140 PRINT "GET SOMEONE ELSE WHO ISN'T SO SMART"
142 PRINT
143 GOTO 30
150 END
```

The numbers in circles on our diagram refer to the following five explanatory notes.

**Notes on the Translation from Extended BASIC
to Minimal BASIC**

1. Many extended BASIC's allow several statements on the same line provided they are separated by colons. To translate, you merely write a separate line for each part. This is what we did with line 20. Other examples are shown in lines 90, 100, 110, 125, and 140.
2. Line 35 shows that many extended BASIC's allow you to omit the word LET.
3. Line 40 shows how a message can be placed within an extended INPUT statement. This translates into a PRINT followed by an INPUT, with the PRINT terminated by a semi-colon.
4. Line 60 shows how the THEN in an IF...THEN statement can be followed by another statement rather than a line number. The translation can be a bit tricky as shown, since ELSE is also used.
5. IF...THEN...ELSE means if true, go to the statement after THEN, if false, go to the statement after ELSE.

Other features of extended BASIC will be introduced in Chapter 4. Techniques for translating them into minimal BASIC will also be shown.

WARNING: When you're finished with a translation make sure that all your "GOTO" and "IF...THEN" statements branch to the correct line numbers. You may have to make some changes.

Here's a sample RUN of the ROULETTE program to show how it should work if you've done the translation properly. Of course runs will differ with different RND generators (and RANDOMIZE routines).

```
    LIST

    RUSSIAN ROULETTE
    --------------------
    TYPE 1 TO SPIN CHAMBER, 0 TO QUIT
    YOUR CHOICE IS? 1
    LOTSALUCK
      BANG!!!   YOU'RE DEAD
    SORRY ABOUT THAT

    NEXT VICTIM PLEASE

    TYPE 1 TO SPIN CHAMBER, 0 TO QUIT
    YOUR CHOICE IS? 1
    LOTSALUCK
    --CLICK--

    YOUR CHOICE IS? 1
    LOTSALUCK
    --CLICK--

    YOUR CHOICE IS? 1
    LOTSALUCK
    --CLICK--

    YOUR CHOICE IS? 1
    LOTSALUCK
    --CLICK--

    YOUR CHOICE IS? 1
    LOTSALUCK
    --CLICK--

    YOUR CHOICE IS? 1
    LOTSALUCK
    --CLICK--

    YOUR CHOICE IS? 1
    LOTSALUCK
    --CLICK--

    YOUR CHOICE IS? 1
    LOTSALUCK
    --CLICK--

    YOUR CHOICE IS? 1
    LOTSALUCK
    --CLICK--

    YOUR CHOICE IS? 1
    LOTSALUCK
    YOU DID IT!!   10 MISSES! -- YOU WIN
    YEA! YEA! YEA! YEA! YEA! YEA! YEA! YEA! YEA! YEA!
    STOP at line 130
```

3
3
3
3
3
3
3
3

SIMPLE COMPUTER
GRAPHICS; SUBSCRIPTED
VARIABLES

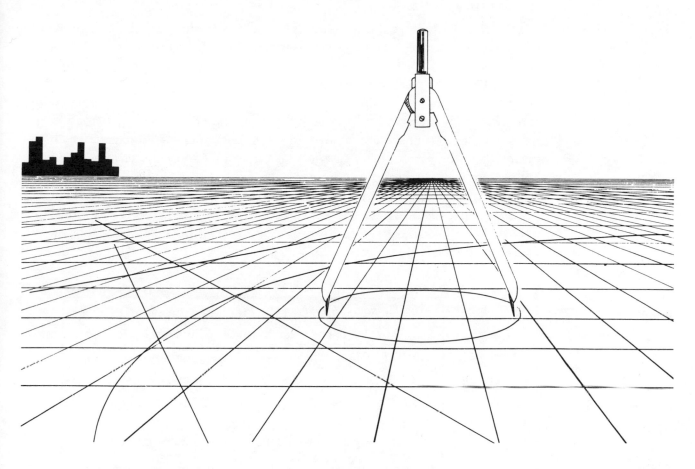

3.0 INTRODUCTION

The ancient wisdom that says "a picture is worth a thousand words" has a special significance for the computer age. With machines that can generate output faster than anyone can read it, there's no doubt that we need new ways to represent this avalanche of data. The best answer (so far) seems to be in computer graphics—sophisticated pictures that show the results of all this computation in a form that is easy to interpret and even easier to remember.

A number of techniques for producing computer graphics will be described in the book. In this chapter, we'll look at simple methods that require only use of a standard "alphanumeric" terminal, either the hard copy or "TV" type. Later chapters will expand on these methods, both in terms of the programs needed to produce graphical displays, and in terms of the hardware required for getting pictures with greater detail.

3.1 Different Kinds of Computer Graphics; Some Terminology

One way to classify computer graphics systems is in terms of the hardware used. A basic distinction that can be made is between "hard copy" (pictures on paper that can be saved for later reference), and "soft copy" (electronic "light" pictures that go away when the machine is shut down). Of course photographs can be taken of soft-copy graphics, but this is not always convenient or easy.

Within each category other distinctions can be made as shown in the chart below. The word "alphanumeric" in the chart means that the terminal can print only standard alphabetic symbols, numbers, and punctuation marks. Some terminals are limited to 64 alphanumeric characters, which means they don't have lower case letters. Other alphanumeric terminals can handle up to 128 characters. However, in both cases, some of these are "control" characters which perform some action (e.g. ring a bell) rather than print anything. By allowing the user to define special characters (e.g. musical notation), an even larger repertoire of symbols can be made available on some alphanumeric terminals.

HARD COPY	H1.	*Standard Alphanumeric Printing Terminals* Usually 10 characters per inch, 6 lines per inch.
	H2.	*Plot-Mode Alphanumeric Printing Terminals* Same as above, plus finer steps for making special shapes out of dots.
	H3.	*X-Y Plotters* Use a pen to make dots, or draw lines connecting any two points.
	H4.	*Other (e.g. Electrostatic, Electrolytic)*
SOFT COPY	S1.	*Cathode-Ray-Tube (CRT) Alphanumeric Displays* Put standard characters on CRT screen.
	S2.	*Raster Scan Color Graphics Displays* Use format similar to home TV (horizontal lines) for both characters and pictures. The entire screen is continuously updated (refreshed).
	S3.	*Cathode-Ray Vector Graphics (also called "stroke writing")* Put characters and/or points and/or continuous lines on CRT screen. Only update (refresh) the parts of the picture being displayed.
	S4.	*Storage Tube Terminals* Put characters, points, and continuous lines on a CRT that does not have to be refreshed.
	S5.	*Dot Matrix Displays* Use a large dot array to get detailed point plots and/or alphanumeric characters.
	S6.	*Other (e.g. futuristic Holographic displays)*

These categories are not exclusive. For example, alphanumeric capability (S1) is frequently found on the other soft copy systems (S2 to S5). And most X-Y plotters (H3) can draw standard characters, often in several styles.

We played it safe and put the word "other" at the end of each list because new ideas keep appearing in the field of graphics. For example, techniques for making hard copies from soft copy terminals already exist. Further down the road, it seems probable that new kinds of thin picture-on-the-wall type color displays will eventually appear for use as both TV and computer display panels. There are even wilder possibilities being explored in the labs, including 3-D holographic projection systems.

For the amateur on a limited budget, the two best bets are currently (1) low-cost alphanumeric terminals (either soft-copy on a TV monitor or hard-copy using a printing mechanism something like an electric typewriter), and (2) graphic systems that use TV-type cathode ray tube (CRT) displays in "raster scan" mode. Vector graphics and dot-matrix displays will also bear investigation when prices come down.

In this chapter we'll look at a number of ways to produce graphics on alphanumeric terminals (H1 and S1). As you'll see, most of the techniques we'll introduce (e.g. scaling) are also applicable to the more advanced graphics systems discussed in Chapter 4.

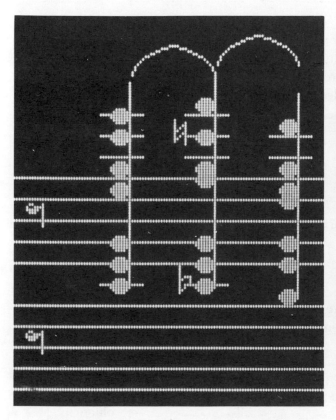

A plasma dot matrix graphics display used with a computer music system.

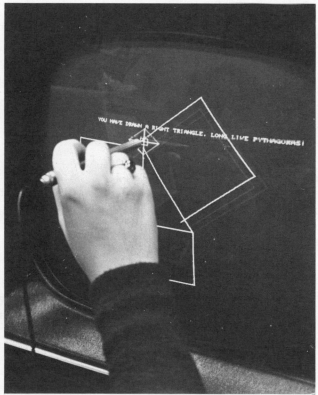

A vector graphics terminal that accepts input from a light pen.

3.2   SIMPLE GRAPHS USING PRINT TAB(X)

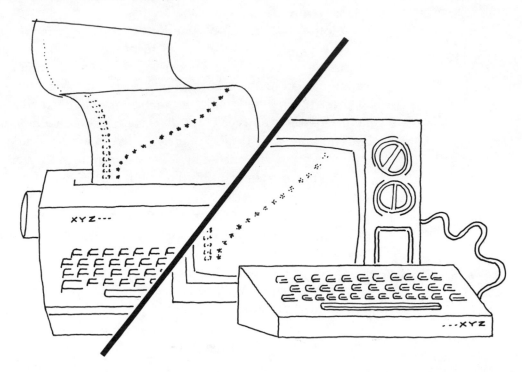

The secret to getting interesting graphical output on an alphanumeric terminal is to find clever ways of controlling the position in which characters print on the paper (or screen) of your terminal. The vertical (up-down) position is usually controlled by the "line-feed" (movement to a new line) that PRINT statements cause. For example, the loop

```
10 FOR X=1 TO 15
20 PRINT "*"
30 NEXT X
```

causes 15 asterisks to print vertically down the left side of the paper. This is because there will be 15 carriage-returns and 15 line-feeds. But if we change line 20 to read

```
20 PRINT TAB(10);"*"
```

something different will happen. The TAB(10) item in the PRINT statement means move *horizontally* ten spaces (0 to 9), and then print the asterisk in the next position (column 10). So now we'll get 15 asterisks printed down the paper, but in column 10.

If we change line 20 further to read

  20 PRINT TAB(X);"*"

the position from the left will change each time around the loop, and we'll get a slanted line of asterisks like this:

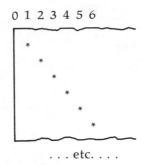

. . . etc. . . .

In other words, TAB(X) means move right to the Xth position before printing the asterisk. (Don't forget—column positions are numbered 0,1,2,3,...).

Now let's get a bit more daring. If we change line 20 to use a more complicated TAB expression like

  20 PRINT TAB(X*X/10);"*"

we'll get a "curved" line. This is because increasing X from 1 to 25 will increase X*X/10 from 0.1 to 62.5. Since TAB uses the integer part of its argument, the asterisks will print in positions determined by the numbers in the third column of the following table.

X	X*X/10	TAB(X*X/10)
1	.1	0
2	.4	0
3	.9	0
4	1.6	1
5	2.5	2
6	3.6	3
7	4.9	4
8	6.4	6
9	8.1	8
10	10.0	10
.	.	.
.	.	.
.	.	.

Mathematicians would say we are plotting a "quadratic" curve. Here's what it looks like:

TAB CURVE

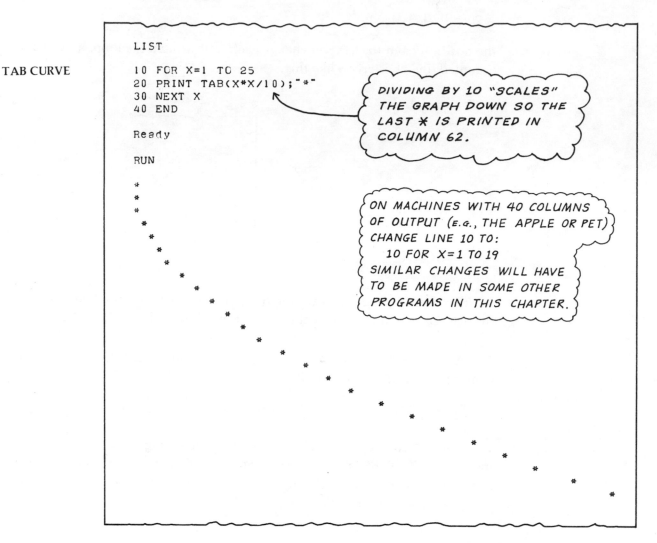

```
LIST

10  FOR X=1 TO 25
20  PRINT TAB(X*X/10);"*"
30  NEXT X
40  END

Ready

RUN
```

DIVIDING BY 10 "SCALES" THE GRAPH DOWN SO THE LAST * IS PRINTED IN COLUMN 62.

ON MACHINES WITH 40 COLUMNS OF OUTPUT (E.G., THE APPLE OR PET) CHANGE LINE 10 TO:
   10 FOR X=1 TO 19
SIMILAR CHANGES WILL HAVE TO BE MADE IN SOME OTHER PROGRAMS IN THIS CHAPTER.

CONFUSION CORNER: The new ANSI standard for BASIC suggests numbering columns 1, 2, 3, . . . etc. However most versions of BASIC follow the 0, 1, 2, 3, . . . scheme we have shown.

TAB can have any legal BASIC expression as its argument, including expressions that use BASIC functions. Here's an example where line 20 prints the symbol "1" in the position determined by TAB(X+3), while line 30 prints the symbol "2" in the position determined by TAB(ABS(3*X-36)+3). The effect is something like graphing the path of two billiard balls. Notice that we are printing the "1" and "2" on alternate lines. (This was done to simplify the program.)

TAB LINES

```
LIST

10  FOR X=0 TO 25
20  PRINT "A:";TAB(X+3);"1"
30  PRINT "B:";TAB(ABS(3*X-36)+3);"2"
40  NEXT X
50  END

Ready

RUN

A:  1
B:                                                  2
A:  1
B:                                            2
A:    1
B:                                        2
A:      1
B:                                    2
A:        1
B:                                2
A:          1
B:                            2
A:            1
B:                        2
A:              1
B:                    2
A:                1
B:                2
A:                  1
B:            2
A:                    1
B:        2
A:                      1
B:    2
A:                        1
B: 2
A:                          1
B:    2
A:                            1
B:        2
A:                              1
B:            2
A:                                1
B:                2
A:                                  1
B:                    2
A:                                    1
B:                        2
A:                                      1
B:                            2
A:                                        1
B:                                2
A:                                          1
B:                                    2
A:                                            1
B:                                        2
A:                                              1
B:                                            2
A:                                                1
B:                                                2
```

Another way to use TAB(X) is to read values of X from data statements. This allows us to print computer graphs that show pictorially what the data "looks" like. For example, we could plot data from the weekly weigh-ins of someone on a reducing diet as follows:

WEIGHT
GRAPH

```
10  PRINT "GRAPH OF WEEKLY WEIGHTS"
20  PRINT "      ";
30  FOR K=100 TO 200 STEP 10:PRINTK;:NEXTK:PRINT
40  PRINT "      ";
50  FOR K= 0 TO 10: PRINT "  +  ";:NEXT K:PRINT
55  LET S = 0
60  FOR X=1 TO 30
70  READ W
80  IF W<0 THEN 150
85  LET S=S+W
90  PRINT X;TAB(4);"I";TAB((W-100)/2+6);"*"
100 NEXT X
110 DATA 155, 149,144, 141, 138, 135, 134.5, 132, 133, 133.7
120 DATA 134, 135, 136, 136, 137, 139, 140.2, 142, 144, 147
130 DATA 150, 143, 135, 130, 126, 123, 121, 120, 119, 119
140 DATA -1
150 PRINT "AVERAGE WEIGHT ="; S/30
160 END

RUN

GRAPH OF WEEKLY WEIGHTS
      100   110   120   130   140   150   160   170   180   190   200
       +     +     +     +     +     +     +     +     +     +     +
    1  I                                    *
    2  I                                 *
    3  I                              *
    4  I                           *
    5  I                          *
    6  I                       *
    7  I                       *
    8  I                      *
    9  I                      *
   10  I                      *
   11  I                      *
   12  I                      *
   13  I                       *
   14  I                       *
   15  I                       *
   16  I                        *
   17  I                         *
   18  I                         *
   19  I                          *
   20  I                           *
   21  I                             *
   22  I                        *
   23  I                     *
   24  I                   *
   25  I                 *
   26  I               *
   27  I              *
   28  I              *
   29  I             *
   30  I             *
AVERAGE WEIGHT = 135.713
```

(Speech bubble pointing to lines 10–50): LINES 10-50 PRINT THE 3 "HEADING" LINES.

(Speech bubble pointing to line 90): THIS LINE PRINTS THE GRAPH. THE FORMULAS USED ARE EXPLAINED IN SECTION 3.4.

One difficulty with our program is that it only gives good graphs for someone with weights in the range of 100 to 200 pounds. We'll return to this program in Section 3.4, and show how to make it automatically adapt to a "personalized" scale of weights. The derivation of the formulas used in line 90 will also be explained there.

3.3   MATHEMATICAL FUNCTIONS IN BASIC

SIN, COS, LOG, EXP, TAN, ATN, SGN

The mysterious words SIN, COS, LOG, EXP, TAN, ATN, SGN are abbreviations for what are called *mathematical functions* (their full names are the "sine", "cosine", "logarithmic", "exponential", "tangent", "arctangent", and "sign" functions). Of course you've already seen the ABS, SQR, and INT functions.

A function can be thought of as a "data crunching" machine. You feed it a piece of input data called the *argument* of the function, and get back output data called the *value* of the function. For example, you can think of the SIN function as working something like this:

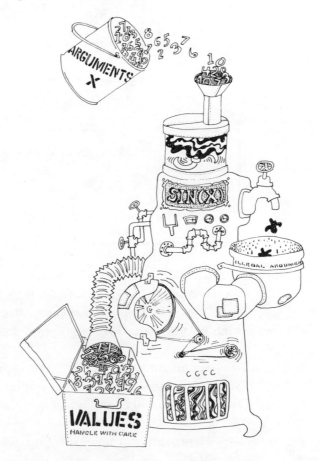

Another way to see what a function does is to make a table. You can do this by writing a program that uses a FOR loop to "plug" different arguments into the function, and then PRINT out the values. Here's such a table for the SIN function:

TABLE

```
LIST

5 PRINT "X", "Y=SIN(X)"
10 FOR X=0 TO 6 STEP 0.5
20 LET Y=SIN(X)
30 PRINT X,Y
40 NEXT X
50 END

Ready

RUN

X                   Y=SIN(X)
 0                  0
 .5                 .479426
 1                  .841471
 1.5               .997495
 2                  .909297
 2.5               .598472
 3                  .14112
 3.5               -.350783
 4                  -.756802
 4.5               -.97753
 5                  -.958924
 5.5               -.70554
 6                  -.279415
```

NOTE: It would be more efficient to replace lines 20 and 30 with one line:

30 PRINT X, SIN(X)

We used two lines just to clarify what was happening.

We won't go very deeply into the mathematical applications of these functions. However they will be extremely useful to us in writing some of the high resolution and color graphics programs described at the end of Chapter 4.

As an introduction to these applications, let's see how we can produce some "pictures" that show graphically what some of the mathematical functions look like, and which are also attractive as design elements.

Here's an example showing what the SIN function looks like when graphed.

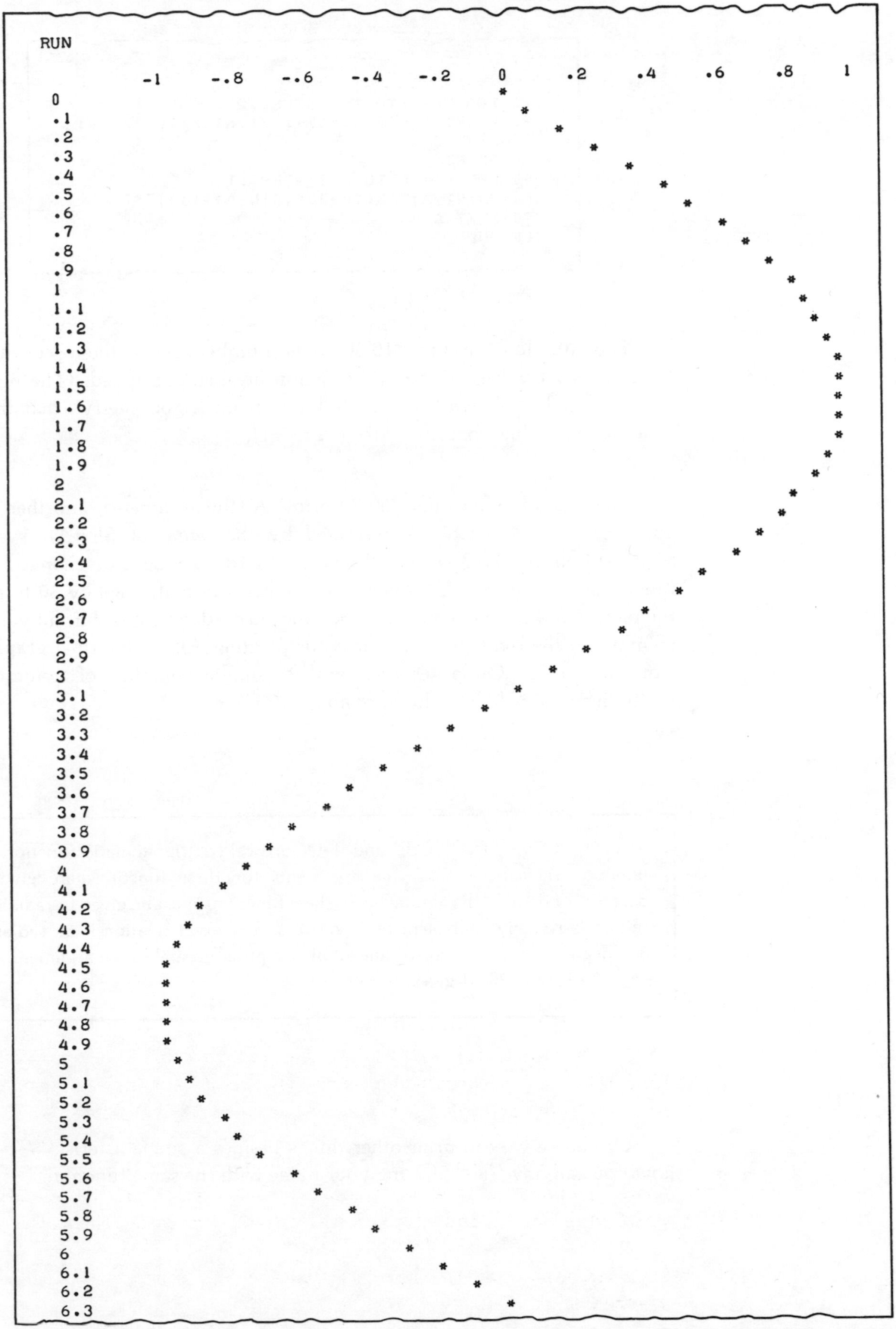
RUN
-1 -.8 -.6 -.4 -.2 0 .2 .4 .6 .8 1
0
.1
.2
.3
.4
.5
.6
.7
.8
.9
1
1.1
1.2
1.3
1.4
1.5
1.6
1.7
1.8
1.9
2
2.1
2.2
2.3
2.4
2.5
2.6
2.7
2.8
2.9
3
3.1
3.2
3.3
3.4
3.5
3.6
3.7
3.8
3.9
4
4.1
4.2
4.3
4.4
4.5
4.6
4.7
4.8
4.9
5
5.1
5.2
5.3
5.4
5.5
5.6
5.7
5.8
5.9
6
6.1
6.2
6.3

SINE GRAPH

```
LIST

10 FOR F=-1 TO 1.1 STEP .2
20 PRINT TAB(9+30*(F+1));INT(F*100)/100;
30 NEXT F
40 PRINT
50 FOR A = 0 TO 6.3 STEP .1
60 PRINT A;TAB(10+30*(SIN(A)+1));"*"
70 NEXT A
80 END
```

The first loop in lines 10-30 puts numbers across the top of the page to show what values of the SIN function are being graphed. (The numbers were selected as shown because we know from trigonometry* that the SIN function has values that range from -1 to +1).

The second loop in lines 50-70 prints A (the *argument*), and then prints an asterisk in a position determined by the *value* of SIN(A). We used SIN(A)+1 in our TAB so that the values -1 to +1 would be changed to the range 0 to 2 (you can't TAB negative values). We multiplied by 30 to spread the picture out from columns 0 to 60, and then added 10 to shift all values 10 columns to the right (to leave room for printing A). So the final graph goes from 10 to 70. On a terminal with a smaller number of columns the multiplier 30 should be reduced to about 15.

MATH NOTE: SIN, COS, and TAN are called trigonomeric functions. In many mathematics books, the arguments for these functions are given in degrees. In BASIC, the arguments of these functions must be given in radians. A radian is roughly equivalent to 57 degrees. The exact relation is 2π radians = 360 degrees. Since 2π = 6.28, line 50 of our program makes the argument A go from 0 to about 360 degrees.

Of course we can print other things besides a single asterisk "*". Here's how you can have fun "SIN"ing your name with the same function.

SINE NAME

```
LIST

10  FOR A=0 TO 6.3 STEP .2
20  LET  Y= SIN(A)
30  PRINT TAB(20*Y+20);"HARVEY KILOBIT"
40  NEXT A
50  END

Ready

RUN

                        HARVEY KILOBIT
                         HARVEY KILOBIT
                           HARVEY KILOBIT
                            HARVEY KILOBIT
                             HARVEY KILOBIT
                              HARVEY KILOBIT
                               HARVEY KILOBIT
                               HARVEY KILOBIT
                               HARVEY KILOBIT
                               HARVEY KILOBIT
                              HARVEY KILOBIT
                             HARVEY KILOBIT
                            HARVEY KILOBIT
                           HARVEY KILOBIT
                          HARVEY KILOBIT
                        HARVEY KILOBIT
                       HARVEY KILOBIT
                      HARVEY KILOBIT
                     HARVEY KILOBIT
                    HARVEY KILOBIT
                   HARVEY KILOBIT
                  HARVEY KILOBIT
                  HARVEY KILOBIT
                  HARVEY KILOBIT
                  HARVEY KILOBIT
                   HARVEY KILOBIT
                    HARVEY KILOBIT
                     HARVEY KILOBIT
                      HARVEY KILOBIT
                       HARVEY KILOBIT
```

The COS function can be used to give similar effects. Both SIN and COS "wiggle" between -1 and +1, but with different starting points. Here's what you'll get when you "COS"ign your name:

COSINE NAME

```
LIST

10  FOR A= 0 TO 6.3 STEP .2
20  LET  Y=COS(A)
30  PRINT TAB(20*Y+20);"HARVEY KILOBIT"
40  NEXT A
50  END


RUN
                              HARVEY KILOBIT
                             HARVEY KILOBIT
                            HARVEY KILOBIT
                           HARVEY KILOBIT
                          HARVEY KILOBIT
                         HARVEY KILOBIT
                        HARVEY KILOBIT
                       HARVEY KILOBIT
                      HARVEY KILOBIT
                     HARVEY KILOBIT
                    HARVEY KILOBIT
                   HARVEY KILOBIT
                  HARVEY KILOBIT
                 HARVEY KILOBIT
                HARVEY KILOBIT
               HARVEY KILOBIT
               HARVEY KILOBIT
               HARVEY KILOBIT
                HARVEY KILOBIT
                 HARVEY KILOBIT
                  HARVEY KILOBIT
                   HARVEY KILOBIT
                    HARVEY KILOBIT
                     HARVEY KILOBIT
                      HARVEY KILOBIT
                       HARVEY KILOBIT
                        HARVEY KILOBIT
                         HARVEY KILOBIT
                          HARVEY KILOBIT
                           HARVEY KILOBIT
                            HARVEY KILOBIT
                             HARVEY KILOBIT
```

Combining functions, and putting multipliers in front of the arguments gives tricky "intermodulation" effects. Here's a pleasing pattern that comes from plotting the combined function Y=COS(2*A) + SIN(A). Electronics buffs will see that we are combining two signals that are "90 degrees out of phase", and that the first one has "twice the frequency" of the second.

MODULATED
NAME

```
LIST

10 FOR A=0 TO 9.5 STEP .2
20 LET Y=COS(2*A)+SIN(A)
30 PRINT TAB(15*Y+30);"HARVEY KILOBIT"
40 NEXT A
50 END

RUN
                                              HARVEY KILOBIT
                                                HARVEY KILOBIT
                                                HARVEY KILOBIT
                                             HARVEY KILOBIT
                                           HARVEY KILOBIT
                                          HARVEY KILOBIT
                                        HARVEY KILOBIT
                                       HARVEY KILOBIT
                                       HARVEY KILOBIT
                                        HARVEY KILOBIT
                                          HARVEY KILOBIT
                                            HARVEY KILOBIT
                                             HARVEY KILOBIT
                                                HARVEY KILOBIT
                                                HARVEY KILOBIT
                                               HARVEY KILOBIT
                                           HARVEY KILOBIT
                                         HARVEY KILOBIT
                                     HARVEY KILOBIT
                                 HARVEY KILOBIT
                            HARVEY KILOBIT
                          HARVEY KILOBIT
                       HARVEY KILOBIT
                       HARVEY KILOBIT
                         HARVEY KILOBIT
                            HARVEY KILOBIT
                               HARVEY KILOBIT
                                  HARVEY KILOBIT
                                    HARVEY KILOBIT
                                       HARVEY KILOBIT
                                         HARVEY KILOBIT
                                            HARVEY KILOBIT
                                            HARVEY KILOBIT
                                           HARVEY KILOBIT
                                         HARVEY KILOBIT
                                       HARVEY KILOBIT
                                      HARVEY KILOBIT
                                      HARVEY KILOBIT
                                       HARVEY KILOBIT
                                         HARVEY KILOBIT
                                            HARVEY KILOBIT
                                              HARVEY KILOBIT
                                                HARVEY KILOBIT
                                                HARVEY KILOBIT
                                               HARVEY KILOBIT
```

Another interesting use of the SIN and COS functions is in the graphing of Lissajous figures (named after the 19th century French physicist, Jules Lissajous). Programs that produce such graphs will be shown in Sections 4.4 and 4.5.

Further information about the graphing of mathematical functions can be found in Chapter 7 of *BASIC and the Personal Computer (Addison Wesley, 1978)*. You can also experiment with other functions in BASIC by using them in a program similar to TABLE (page 110). However, you will find that for some arguments, you may get error messages. For example, SQR and LOG cannot have negative arguments. Another trouble-maker is TAN. For example, TAN (3.14159265/2) has the value "infinity", so computers can't handle it, and will produce either nonsense or some kind of error message. The best way to identify such cases is to read about these functions in a mathematics book, and then experiment with printing tables of the type shown at the beginning of Section 3.3.

3.4   WHAT TO DO IF YOUR BASIC DOESN'T HAVE TAB; THE SCALING OF GRAPHS

Some of the simpler versions of BASIC may not allow TAB, or they may only allow TAB with a constant (like TAB(5)). You can simulate a statement like

```
30 PRINT TAB(Y);"*"
```

by replacing it with a loop that prints Y blanks, and then follows this with a statement that prints an asterisk on the same line. Here's the code for simulating 30 PRINT TAB(Y);"*"

```
30 FOR T=0 TO Y-1
40 PRINT " ";
50 NEXT T
60 PRINT "*"
```

We let the variable T go from zero to Y-1 because columns on a printer are numbered with zero as the starting position. A program to print a graph of the SIN function using this trick would look like the following:

SIMULATED TAB

```
LIST

10 FOR A = 0 TO 6.8 STEP .2
20 LET Y=INT(30*SIN(A)+30)
30 FOR T=0 TO Y-1
40 PRINT " ";
50 NEXT T
60 PRINT "*"
70 NEXT A
80 END

Ready

RUN
```

THIS LOOP SIMULATES USING TAB(Y);

Scaling Graphs

You've seen that although the SIN function has values that go from -1 to +1, we were able to spread the graph out over 60 columns. We did this by first adding +1 (which is called *translating* the range of values). This was done to avoid negative numbers, giving a range of values 0 to 2 instead. Then we multiplied by 30 (which is called *scaling* the range of values) so that the range became 0 to 60. In this way we were able to spread 2 units over 60 terminal columns. We can either say that our "scale factor" was 30 terminal spaces per mathematical unit, or conversely, that it was 1/30 of a mathematical unit per terminal space.

Let's now return to the dieter's weight graphing program from Section 3.1 and see how we can add an automatic scaling feature. The diet program was supposed to graph weights from 100 to 200 pounds. To make the left edge of the paper correspond to 100 pounds (instead of zero), the first thing we did was "shift" the whole graph left 100 units. This was done by subtracting 100 from W (a translation).

Our next decision was to scale the weights from 100 to 200 into 50 terminal spaces. To do this we multiplied by a scale factor of

$50/(200-100) = 1/2$ terminal space per pound

Example: For a weight of 150 pounds, the program should first translate this weight by taking 150-100=50. It should then scale it by taking 50 * (1/2) = 25 terminal spaces. Here's a picture of what happens:

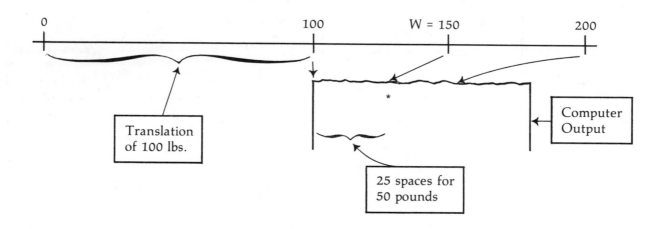

All of this can be done by saying

PRINT TAB ((W-100)*(1/2));"*"

But multiplying by 1/2 is the same as dividing by 2, so this can be written more simply as

PRINT TAB ((W-100)/2);"*"

To improve the readability of the graph, we then allowed six extra spaces for printing X (the week number) followed by the symbol "I" in column 4. Putting all these things together gave line 90 of the original program:

90 PRINT X;TAB(4);"I";TAB((W-100)/2+6);"*"

Thus for X=21 and W=150 we'd have

Col.   0123456789......................31 (= 25 + 6)

```
    20  I
    21  I                          *
         .
         .
         .
```

Automatic Scaling

We can generalize this idea by using a starting weight called A (instead of 100), and a final weight called B (instead of 200). This makes the scale factor 50/(B-A) spaces per pound. The translation is now A pounds (not 100), and the starting weight at the left edge of the graph is W-A (not W-100). This gives us as a generalized print statement:

460 PRINT X;TAB(4);"I";TAB((W-A)*(50/(B-A))+6);"*"

It will also be necessary to generalize the headings at the top of the graph, and this is done in a similar manner. Here's a program that does this "customized" scaling in a subroutine (lines 315 to 480). The first time the subroutine is used, the weights go from 100 to 200 (line 180). But then the user is asked to supply a more personalized set of minimum and maximum weights. These are input as A and B in lines 280 to 301. This program also contains the user's "goal" weight as the first number in DATA statement 900. This way the program can tell the dieter how many "pounds-to-goal" there are. The -1 the the end of the DATA is used to stop the READ loop (see line 80). Here's the improved program and a run.

SCALED
WEIGHT
GRAPH

```
LIST

10 PRINT"WEIGHT WATCHER'S RECORD"
20 PRINT:PRINT"WEEK","WEIGHT","WT. LOSS"
30 S=0: D=0
35 REM-----CALC. & PRINT TABLE----------
40 READ G
45 I=0
50 I=I+1
60 READ W
70 IF I=1 THEN 110
80 IF W<0 THEN 140
90 D=W1-W
100 S=S+D
110 PRINT I,W,D
120 W1=W
130 GOTO 50
140 PRINT:PRINT"AVG. WEEKLY LOSS   ";S/(I-1);"LBS."
150 PRINT"LBS. TO GOAL  ";W1-G
160 PRINT"TOTAL POUNDS LOST SO FAR  ";S
170 PRINT:PRINT"WEIGHT WATCHER'S GRAPH":PRINT
175 REM-----STANDARD SCALE(100-200)-----
180 A=100:B=200
190 GOSUB 315
250 REM-----CUSTOMIZED SCALE----------
260 PRINT:PRINT"WANT A CUSTOMIZED GRAPH";:INPUT A$
270 IF A$="NO" THEN 999
280 PRINT"WHAT IS THE SMALLEST NUMBER YOU WANT(INSTEAD OF 100)";
290 INPUT A
300 PRINT"WHAT IS THE LARGEST NUMBER YOU WANT(INSTEAD OF 200)";
301 INPUT B
303 GOSUB 315
305 PRINT"WANT ANOTHER GRAPH";:INPUT A$
307 IF A$="YES" THEN 280
309 GOTO 999
315 REM-----GRAPH SUBROUTINE-----
316 X=0
317 REM-----HEADING (LINE 1)-----
330 FOR I=A TO B STEP 10
340 PRINT TAB(X*50*(10/(B-A))+5);I;
350 X=X+1
360 NEXT I
370 PRINT
375 REM-----HEADING (LINE 2)-----
380 PRINT"    I";
390 FOR I=0 TO (X-1)
400 PRINT TAB(I*50*(10/(B-A))+7);"+";
410 NEXT I
420 PRINT
425 RESTORE
426 READ G
428 REM-----PRINT GRAPH-----
429 I=0
430 I=I+1
440 READ W
450 IF W<0 THEN 480
460 PRINT I;TAB(4);"I";TAB((W-A)*(50/(B-A))+6);"*"
470 GOTO 430
480 RETURN
900 DATA 122,153,149.5,147.5,147.5,145,144.5,141,141.5,139.25
910 DATA 139.5,137.5,138.5,-1
999 END
```

> SUBROUTINE 315-480 IS USED FOR BOTH THE STANDARD AND CUSTOMIZED SCALES. THE VALUES OF A AND B MAKE THE DIFFERENCE.

```
RUN
WEIGHT WATCHER'S RECORD

WEEK           WEIGHT          WT. LOSS
 1             153             0
 2             149.5           3.5
 3             147.5           2
 4             147.5           0
 5             145             2.5
 6             144.5           .5
 7             141             3.5
 8             141.5           -.5
 9             139.25          2.25
10             139.5           -.25
11             137.5           2
12             138.5           -1


AVG. WEEKLY LOSS    1.20833 LBS.
LBS. TO GOAL    16.5
TOTAL POUNDS LOST SO FAR    14.5

WEIGHT WATCHER'S GRAPH

        100   110   120   130   140   150   160   170   180   190   200
    I    +     +     +     +     +     +     +     +     +     +     +
 1  I                                 *
 2  I                              *
 3  I                               *
 4  I                               *
 5  I                              *
 6  I                              *
 7  I                            *
 8  I                            *
 9  I                           *
10  I                           *
11  I                         *
12  I                          *
```

THE SECOND GRAPH SHOWS THE SAME DATA AS THE FIRST, BUT IT IS SPREAD OUT OVER A BETTER RANGE.

```
WANT A CUSTOMIZED GRAPH? YES
WHAT IS THE SMALLEST NUMBER YOU WANT(INSTEAD OF 100)? 130
WHAT IS THE LARGEST NUMBER YOU WANT(INSTEAD OF 200)? 150
        130                         140                         150
    I    +                           +                           +
 1  I                                                              *
 2  I                                                    *
 3  I                                                 *
 4  I                                                 *
 5  I                                           *
 6  I                                        *
 7  I                              *
 8  I                                *
 9  I                           *
10  I                           *
11  I                         *
12  I                          *
WANT ANOTHER GRAPH? NO
```

3.5   SUBSCRIPTED VARIABLES

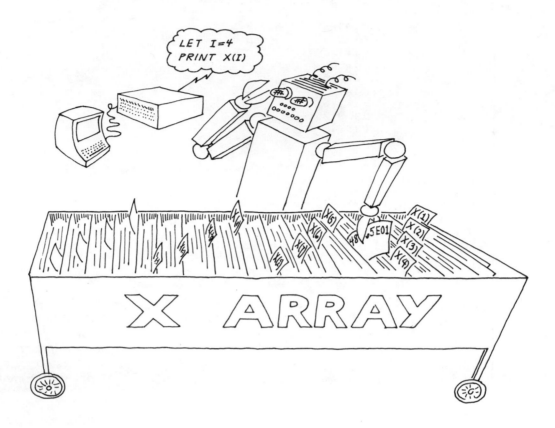

So far we have been limited to variable names made up of a single letter (A,B,C...,Z), or a single letter followed by a single digit (A1, A2, A3,...Z8,Z9). One of the problems you eventually run into with such variables is that you can't always foresee how many are needed, and there's no way for the computer to add new variable names when this happens. To see what the problem is, look at the next program which asks a person to input an unspecified number of weights.

Since we don't know how many weights the person may type in, we ask the user to type zero to signal when input is finished. Since we want to print "deviations from the average" of each weight, we'll have to save all the weights in separate variables until the end (because only then can we calculate the average). So we "guess" that at most four weights will be input, and use separate input statements to save these weights in W1, W2, W3, and W4. As you can see this is a very clumsy and very limited approach. We also get a ridiculous "deviation from the average" when the user types in the zero. The villain here is line 220 which blindly prints *all* the differences.

HORRIBLE
EXAMPLE

```
LIST

10 LET S=0
20 PRINT"TYPE A WEIGHT AFTER EACH ? --TYPE 0 WHEN FINISHED"
30 INPUT W1
40 IF W1=0 THEN 190
50 N=N+1
60 S=S+W1
70 INPUT W2
80 IF W2=0 THEN 190
90 N=N+1
100 S=S+W2
110 INPUT W3
120 IF W3=0 THEN 190
130 N=N+1
140 S=S+W3
150 INPUT W4
160 IF W4=0 THEN 190
170 N=N+1
180 S=S+W4
190 LET A=S/N
200 PRINT "AVERAGE WEIGHT =";A
210 PRINT "DEVIATIONS FROM THE AVERAGE WERE"
220 PRINT W1-A;W2-A;W3-A;W4-A
230 END
OK

RUN
TYPE A WEIGHT AFTER EACH ? --TYPE 0 WHEN FINISHED
? 150
? 175
? 163
? 0
AVERAGE WEIGHT = 162.667
DEVIATIONS FROM THE AVERAGE WERE
-12.6667  12.3333   .333328 -162.667
OK
```

HERE'S JUST ONE OF THE REASONS THIS IS A POOR PROGRAM.

There's got to be a better way! And there is. The new feature that clears up this problem is the ability of BASIC to have what are called "subscripted variables". These look like the following:

A(1), A(2), A(3), A(4),...Z(86), Z(87), Z(88),...

You use a variable name followed by any positive integer placed in parentheses. A(3) is pronounced "A sub 3", and it really means the third location in an *array* of locations. You can have hundreds (or even thousands) of these locations, depending on how much memory your computer has.

What's an array? It's a concept that allows you to organize your computer's memory in blocks of variables that look something like this:

A(0)	data
A(1)	data
A(2)	data
A(3)	data
A(4)	data
Z(0)	data
Z(1)	data
Z(2)	data
•	•
•	•
•	•
Z(87)	data
Z(88)	data

How many variables are in each block is up to you. You let the program know by using the DIMension statement as follows:

10 DIM A(4), Z(88)

This means reserve a block of five subscripted variables with names from A(0) to A(4), and a block of 89 with names Z(0) to Z(88).

NOTE: (1) If you don't use DIM, BASIC will assume you meant DIM A(10), Z(10). (2) Some BASIC's don't allow the A(0) or Z(0) names, so they give you one less location in each block than our diagram shows.

And Now for the Really Good News!

The power of arrays (or blocks) of subscripted variables is that the computer can reference them through use of program variables. This is because you can also use *variables* as subscripts. Watch carefully:

ARRAY DEMO

```
LIST

5 DIM W(100)
10 INPUT "HOW MANY WEIGHTS";N
12 PRINT "TYPE A WEIGHT AFTER EACH ?"
15 FOR K = 1 TO N
20 INPUT W(K)
25 NEXT K
30 PRINT "YOUR WEIGHTS IN REVERSE ORDER ARE"
40 FOR K = N TO 1 STEP -1
50 PRINT W(K)
60 NEXT K
70 END

Ready

RUN

HOW MANY WEIGHTS? 4
TYPE A WEIGHT AFTER EACH ?
? 234
? 211
? 213
? 189
YOUR WEIGHTS IN REVERSE ORDER ARE
 189
 213
 211
 234
```

The secret to understanding what happened in this program is to picture memory as follows:

N	4
W(1)	234
W(2)	211
W(3)	213
W(4)	189
W(5)	
•	
•	
•	
W(100)	

In the loop 15 to 25, the user put numbers in the four locations W(1), W(2), W(3), and W(4), so the loop 50 to 70 has no trouble printing them out in reverse (or any other) order. This is because it can reference W(I) for any sequence of I's. The computer can now find variables under *program control*.

WARNING: W(3) is very different from W3. Don't get these confused. Also note that you can use W(K) in a program, but WK is illegal in minimal BASIC.

A program that uses subscripted variables is much more flexible since it can "decide" which variables to manipulate by using a variable for the subscript—like the K and J in W(K) or W(J). Let's see how this idea can make our weight deviation program much more useful.

WEIGHT AVERAGE

```
LIST

10 DIM W(100)
20 LET S=0
30 PRINT "HOW MANY WEIGHTS TO BE AVERAGED";
40 INPUT N
50 PRINT "TYPE A WEIGHT AFTER EACH ?"
60 FOR K=1 TO N
70 INPUT W(K)
80 LET S=S+W(K)
90 NEXT K
95 LET A=S/N
100 PRINT "AVERAGE WEIGHT =";A
110 PRINT "DEVIATIONS FROM THE AVERAGE WERE"
120 FOR K=1 TO N
130 PRINT W(K)-A
140 NEXT K
150 PRINT
160 END

Ready

RUN

HOW MANY WEIGHTS TO BE AVERAGED? 6
TYPE A WEIGHT AFTER EACH ?
? 175
? 163
? 181
? 145
? 162
? 150
AVERAGE WEIGHT = 162.667
DEVIATIONS FROM THE AVERAGE WERE
  12.3333
  .333333
  18.3333
 -17.6667
 -.666667
 -12.6667
```

THIS LOOP PRODUCES THE QUESTION MARKS THAT PROMPT FOR INPUT TO THE W ARRAY.

N	6
W(1)	175
W(2)	163
W(3)	181
W(4)	145
W(5)	162
W(6)	150
•	•
•	•
•	•
W(100)	

K=3 → W(3)
K=6 → W(6)

Notice how easy it is to get the deviations in line 130. This is because the FOR loop of line 120 controls the subscript K. You should think of K as though it were a *pointer*, moving down the list of weights, automatically selecting each in turn until it reaches the Nth one. (N=6 in our example, but it could be as high as 100).

You can have several arrays in a program. (Of course each array uses as many memory locations as you dimension, so you may run out of space unless you have a lot of memory in your machine). Here's an improvement on the previous program that uses two arrays with 100 locations each. This program also contains a useful idea in the subroutine (lines 1000 to 1070). It's an algorithm for finding the largest (max) and smallest (min) item stored in an array. It works by first assuming that W(1) is both the largest (L=W(1)) and smallest (S=W(1)) item. Then it loops down through the array, looking at all the remaining items. If it finds a W(K) that's smaller (line 1020), then *this* W(K) goes into S. Also, we "remember" which subscript corresponded to the latest "smallest" with the variable Y (see line 1050). The same thing is done to find the largest W(K) in lines 1022 and 1030. The subscript of the largest weight is "remembered" with X. Then X and Y can be used to point at the months in which largest and smallest weights occurred (see lines 110 and 120).

MAX-MIN
WEIGHTS

```
LIST

5 DIM W(100),M(100)
10 PRINT "HOW MANY MONTHLY WEIGHTS TO BE AVERAGED";
20 INPUT N
30 PRINT "AFTER EACH ? TYPE MONTH #, WEIGHT"
40 LET S=0
50 FOR I=1 TO N
60 INPUT M(I),W(I)
70 LET S=S+W(I)
80 NEXT I
90 PRINT "AVERAGE WEIGHT WAS";S/N
100 GOSUB 1000
110 PRINT "YOUR LARGEST WEIGHT WAS ";L;"LBS. IN MONTH # ";M(X)
120 PRINT "YOUR SMALLEST WEIGHT WAS ";S;"LBS. IN MONTH # ";M(Y)
130 STOP
999 REM---ROUTINE TO FIND MAX WT., MIN WT., AND CORRESPONDING MONTHS"---
1000 LET L=W(1):LET S=W(1):LET X=1:LET Y=1
1010 FOR K=2 TO N
1020 IF W(K)<S THEN 1050
1022 IF W(K)>L THEN 1030
1024 GOTO 1060
1030 LET L=W(K):LET X=K
1040 GOTO 1060
1050 LET S=W(K):LET Y=K
1060 NEXT K
1070 RETURN
9000 END
```

X AND Y WILL "POINT" AT THE MAXIMUM AND MINIMUM WEIGHTS WHEN THIS LOOP FINISHES.

```
RUN

HOW MANY MONTHLY WEIGHTS TO BE AVERAGED? 5
AFTER EACH ? TYPE MONTH #, WEIGHT
? 4,170
? 5,175
? 6,189
? 7,182
? 8,173
AVERAGE WEIGHT WAS 177.8
YOUR LARGEST WEIGHT WAS   189 LBS. IN MONTH #  6
YOUR SMALLEST WEIGHT WAS  170 LBS. IN MONTH #  4
STOP at line 130
```

The preceding program handles the weights for one person nicely. But suppose you want to keep records for a group of people, and use your program to select and average the data for any one of them. This suggests that it would be nice to have variables with two subscripts, one to "point" out the month, the other to "point" out the person. In other words, we'd like to use a variable like $W(5,4)$ to mean the weight in the 5th month of person #4. This can be done in most versions of BASIC, using two-dimensional arrays. Let's see how they work.

Two-Dimensional Arrays; Double Subscripts

In addition to one-dimensional arrays, it's also possible to set aside two-dimensional or rectangular arrays (blocks) of memory in most versions of BASIC. For example,

10 DIM A(5,4)

means reserve a block of 20 computer memory locations called

$A(1,1)$ $A(1,2)$,..., $A(5,3)$, $A(5,4)$.

You should picture these memory locations as being organized in a block with five rows and four columns as following:

A(1,1) (data)	A(1,2) (data)	A(1,3) (data)	A(1,4) (data)
A(2,1) (data)	A(2,2) (data)	A(2,3) (data)	A(2,4) (data)
A(3,1) (data)	A(3,2) (data)	A(3,3) (data)	A(3,4) (data)
A(4,1) (data)	A(4,2) (data)	A(4,3) (data)	A(4,4) (data)
A(5,1) (data)	A(5,2) (data)	A(5,3) (data)	A(5,4) (data)

I=3

J=2

Again the real power of these "doubly-subscripted" variables is that the subscripts themselves can be variables. We can now write A(I,J) to "point" at the data in row I and column J. If I=3 and J=2, the program will use the data in A(3,2). So this would be a natural way to store the weight of member #2 for month #3 in a diet program. But of course there are many other uses. A more ambitious application will be explained in Chapter 4 where we'll show how a two-dimensional array is a natural way of storing the data for a business record sorting program.

For a quick example now, here's a program which prints a table of how many sales of each of three items were made in four months. In other words, our picture of the data structure is the following:

	ITEM 1	ITEM 2	ITEM 3
Month 1	345	687	149
Month 2	344	689	235
Month 3	378	499	245
Month 4	377	568	388

In this example think of ROW as meaning "MONTH", and COLUMN as meaning "ITEM". The main thing to observe is that two nested FOR loops are needed for both INPUT (lines 60 to 110) and OUTPUT (lines 150 to 200). The outer loop on I controls the row subscript, while the inner loop on J controls the column subscript. The comma at the end of line 170 forces all the items controlled by the J loop to print on one line. The PRINT statement in line 190 produces a carriage return and line feed to get ready for the next time the J loop is executed.

ARRAY DEMO 2

```
LIST

10 DIM D(10,4)
20 PRINT "HOW MANY ROWS OF DATA";
30 INPUT M
40 PRINT "HOW MANY COLUMNS PER ROW";
50 INPUT N
60 FOR I=1 TO M
70 PRINT "TYPE";N; "ITEMS FOR ROW";I        ⎤
80 FOR J=1 TO N                             │
90 INPUT D(I,J)                             │  ← ARRAY INPUT
100 NEXT J                                  │
110 NEXT I                                  ⎦
120 PRINT "DATA SUMMARY"
130 FOR I=1 TO N:PRINT "ITEM";I,:NEXT I:PRINT
140 PRINT"----------------------------------"
150 FOR I=1 TO M                            ⎤
160 FOR J=1 TO N                            │
170 PRINT D(I,J),                           │  ← ARRAY OUTPUT
180 NEXT J                                  │
190 PRINT                                   │
200 NEXT I                                  ⎦
210 END
```

```
RUN

HOW MANY ROWS OF DATA? 4
HOW MANY COLUMNS PER ROW? 3
TYPE 3 ITEMS FOR ROW 1
? 345
? 687
? 149
TYPE 3 ITEMS FOR ROW 2
? 344
? 689
? 235
TYPE 3 ITEMS FOR ROW 3
? 378
? 499
? 245
TYPE 3 ITEMS FOR ROW 4
? 377
? 568
? 388
DATA SUMMARY
ITEM 1          ITEM 2          ITEM 3
-------------------------------------
  345             687             149
  344             689             235
  378             499             245
  377             568             388
```

This program doesn't do very much at present, but we'll return to a discussion of two-dimensional arrays in Section 4.1, and show another example of their use in Section 4.3.

SELF-TEST

1. Simulate running the following program on paper, and then check your results on a computer.

```
10 LET A(1)=1
20 LET A(2)=1
30 PRINT A(1);
40 PRINT A(2);
50 FOR K = 3 TO 10
60 LET A(K) = A(K-1) + A(K-2)
70 PRINT A(K);
80 NEXT K
100 PRINT "END OF FIBONACCI DEMO"
110 END
```

2. Simulate running this program, writing the output you'd expect on paper, along with the proper spacing. Then try it on a computer.

```
10 FOR I = 1 TO 3
20 FOR J = 1 TO 4
30 LET A(I,J) = I * J
40 PRINT A(I,J);
50 NEXT J
60 PRINT
70 NEXT I
80 END
```

3.6 BAR GRAPHS; PINBALL SIMULATION

Graphical output is often useful in displaying the results of what are called "computer simulations". These are programs that make the computer imitate some other process. Simulations are a good way to study complex processes before trying the real thing.

Our simulation program will imitate a pinball machine with rigid (non-moving) pins on a slanted table, and pockets at the bottom. The program "drops" balls in the opening indicated by the arrow. As each simulated ball rolls down, it strikes pins and bounces randomly to the left or right, finally landing in one of the pockets.

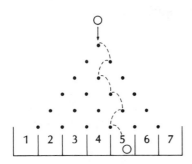

We would like to know how many balls end up in each pocket after a large number of trials. One way to find out would be to build the pinball machine and spend days rolling balls and counting how many land in each pocket. Instead, let's write a program to simulate such a machine. We'll use seven pockets in our example.

To begin with, let's set up a "pointer" P which describes where the ball is at any given time. Another way to explain P is to say it points at the pcoket position directly under the ball. At the beginning of the simulation, the ball would fall into pocket 4 if no pins were in the way, so we'll start by setting P = 4. Since there are 6 levels of pins, we'll need a loop "FOR L = 1 TO 6" to simulate the entire drop. At each level, the ball will hit a pin and bounce either to the left or to the right.

This is random process, so let's use random numbers to decide the ball's path. If the ball does hit a pin we'll assume it's knocked one-half pocket to either side, that is, we'll assume the pins are always in the middle of the ball's path. We'll set P = P + .5 or P = P - .5, depending on which direction the ball goes. When the ball finally lands in a pocket we'll keep score by adding one to that pocket's contents. Then we'll drop the next ball. After all the balls have been dropped, we'll print a table of pockets and the corresponding number of balls.

PINBALL COUNT

```
100  REM---PUT RANDOMIZE STATEMENT HERE IF NEEDED
110  FOR N=1 TO 7
120      LET C(N)=0
130  NEXT N
140  PRINT "POCKET","COUNT"
160  FOR B=1 TO 100
170      LET P=4
180      FOR L=1 TO 6
190          LETX=RND(1)
200          IF X<.5 THEN 230
210          LET P=P-.5
220          GOTO 240
230          LET P=P+.5
240      NEXT L
250      LET C(P)=C(P)+1
260  NEXT B
270  FOR N=1 TO 7
280      PRINT N, C(N)
290  NEXT N
300  END
```

NOTICE HOW THE POINTER P IS ALSO USED AS A SUBSCRIPT; THIS MAKES THE VARIABLE C(P) COUNT THE NUMBER OF BALLS FALLING INTO THE POCKET TO WHICH P FINALLY POINTS.

'IN BASIC-PLUS 3 LINES LIKE THIS CAN BE
'WRITTEN AS 1 BY USING A 'FOR MODIFIER':
'270 PRINT N, C(N)   FOR N=1 TO 7

```
RUN
POCKET          COUNT
  1               0
  2               9
  3              19
  4              35
  5              25
  6               8
  7               4
OK
  RUN
POCKET          COUNT
  1               1
  2               7
  3              21
  4              37
  5              24
  6               7
  7               3
OK
RUN
POCKET          COUNT
  1               4
  2               4
  3              23
  4              33
  5              25
  6               8
  7               3
OK
```

You can see that most of the balls land in pockets 3, 4, and 5. If we plot the distribution of balls, we get a graph something like this:

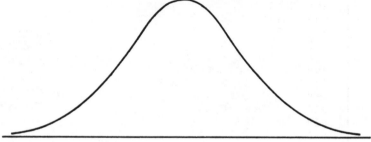

```
35              x
30          x   x
# BALLS  25
20
15      x       x
10
 5
        1 2 3 4 5 6 7
           POCKETS
```

This is a rather crude graph. Theoretically, the graph should approximate what is called a "normal" or bell-shaped curve that looks like this:

To get a better approximation to this curve, we'll have to run more trials. Suppose we change our program so there are 31 pockets with pins at 30 levels, and drop 5,000 balls into this pinball machine. Let's also make our program graph the results.

For this problem, a good way to display results is to use a histogram, or bar graph. Here's a short program segment that illustrates the basic technique needed for making a bar-graph on an alphanumeric terminal. Suppose we wanted to graph the contents of 3 pockets that had 50, 110, and 87 balls each. Here's what we could do:

BAR GRAPH

```
LIST

10 LET C(1) = 50
20 LET C(2) = 110
30 LET C(3) = 87
40 FOR I =1  TO 3
45 PRINT I; TAB(5);C(I);TAB(10);"I";
50 FOR K=1 TO C(I)/10
60 PRINT "<*>";
70 NEXT K
80 PRINT
90 NEXT I
100 END

Ready

RUN

   1    50   I<*><*><*><*><*>
   2   110   I<*><*><*><*><*><*><*><*><*><*><*>
   3    87   I<*><*><*><*><*><*><*><*>
```

The loop 50-60-70 prints one "bar" in our bar graph, using the symbol <*> for every 10 balls that reach pocket C(I). The outer loop 40-90 controls the number of bars, one for each pocket.

SELF-TEST

1. Write a program that displays the results of dropping 5,000 balls in a pinball machine with 31 pockets. Print one graphing symbol (say "0") for every 10 balls if you're using a 72 column terminal, or one symbol for every 20 balls on a 40 column terminal. The output should look something like that in the sample run we've shown.

WARNING: This program will take a long time to run!

```
RUN

PKT COUNT GRAPH

  1    0 :
  2    0 :
  3    0 :
  4    0 :
  5    0 :
  6    0 :
  7    4 :
  8   10 :0
  9   23 :00
 10   61 :000000
 11  148 :00000000000000
 12  248 :000000000000000000000000
 13  407 :00000000000000000000000000000000000000000
 14  604 :000000000000000000000000000000000000000000000000000000000000
 15  644 :00000000000000000000000000000000000000000000000000000000000000000
 16  719 :000000000000000000000000000000000000000000000000000000000000000000000000
 17  640 :0000000000000000000000000000000000000000000000000000000000000000
 18  578 :0000000000000000000000000000000000000000000000000000000000
 19  418 :000000000000000000000000000000000000000000
 20  240 :000000000000000000000000
 21  151 :000000000000000
 22   62 :000000
 23   28 :00
 24   10 :0
 25    5 :
 26    0 :
 27    0 :
 28    0 :
 29    0 :
 30    0 :
 31    0 :
```

3.7   PRINT USING; FRACTURED FRACTIONS

Some extended versions of BASIC permit what is called "formated" output. This means that you can specify the format (or arrangement) of items in a line of output, and avoid some of the limitations of the "standard" spacing for numbers and characters. In particular, you can specify the number of decimal digits to be printed, the position of the decimal, the size of the field, and the position of the digits within that field. Here's a simple example that shows how it works.

```
10 LET A$= "   ###.####"
20 PRINT USING A$; 355/113
30 END
OK
RUN
      3.1416
```

We left room for 3 digits, a decimal, and 4 more digits
We forced two spaces at the beginning of the "field"

Thus the field we specified is 10 positions wide.

In line 10 we used what's called a string variable, A$. This is a variable in which characters are stored instead of numbers. The characters to be stored are placed between quotation marks. In our example, the string A$ consists of two blanks, three pound signs (#), a decimal, and four more pound signs. The blanks (or spaces) force spaces in the output field, while the pound signs say exactly how many positions are available for digits before and after the decimal.

If you wish, the two parts of PRINT USING can be written as a single statement:

10 PRINT USING "   ###.####"; 355/113

There are other symbols that can be included in the format string, allowing things like $, *, or spaces to be made part of the output. Since these features are not standardized, you'll have to read your own BASIC reference manual to get further detail.

The PRINT USING and the TAB statements complement each other, allowing you to produce just about any kind of output format. Let's look at an example that illustrates how both features might be used in the same program.

Fractured Fractions

You have probably seen the fraction 22/7 used as an approximation for PI, correct to 3 significant figures. The example just given used 355/113 as a much better approximation. This raises the question of whether we could find a fraction that does even better. A more general question is this: can we find fractions that approximate any decimal number to any required accuracy?

An Algorithm for Finding Approximating Fractions

The answer is that we *can* find fractions which produce decimal numbers to any degree of accuracy. (However, if we use a computer, then there will be a limit on accuracy imposed by the BASIC interpreter, which may not handle more than 6 or 7 significant figures. To go beyond this limit requires software with "multiple precision" arithmetic. Our example will illustrate this by showing what happens on a system that allows 15 significant digits.)

The algorithm we'll use first generates what are called continued fractions, which are like fractions within fractions within fractions, etc.

General Algorithm	*Example*
Y_0 is the decimal we start with	$Y_0 = 2.55$
Let R_0 = the integer part of Y_0	$R_0 = 2$
$Y_1 = \dfrac{1}{Y_0 - R_0}$	$Y_1 = \dfrac{1}{2.55 - 2} = \dfrac{1}{.55} = 1.81818\ldots$
$R_1 = \text{INT}(Y_1)$	$R_1 = 1$
$Y_2 = \dfrac{1}{Y_1 - R_1}$	$Y_2 = \dfrac{1}{1.818\ldots - 1} = \dfrac{1}{.81818\ldots} = 1.222\ldots$
$R_2 = \text{INT}(Y_2)$	$R_2 = 1$
$Y_3 = \dfrac{1}{Y_2 - R_2}$	$Y_3 = \dfrac{1}{1.222\ldots - 1} = \dfrac{1}{.222\ldots} = 4.5000$
$R_3 = \text{INT}(Y_3)$	$R_3 = 4$
In general, $R_i = \text{INT}(Y_i)$	$Y_4 = \dfrac{1}{4.5 - 4} = \dfrac{1}{.5} = 2$
$Y_{i+1} = \dfrac{1}{Y_i - R_i}$	$R_4 = 2$

Since $R_4 = Y_4$ we have gone as far as we can.

The continued fraction then looks like this:

$$Y_0 = R_0 + \cfrac{1}{R_1 + \cfrac{1}{R_2 + \cfrac{1}{R_3 + \cdots \cfrac{1}{R_n}}}}$$

$$2.55 = 2 + \cfrac{1}{1 + \cfrac{1}{1 + \cfrac{1}{4 + \cfrac{1}{2}}}}$$

Since a continued fraction is hard to use, we must next convert it to a simple fraction. This is done by starting at the bottom and working up, using a second algorithm as follows:

$$4 + \frac{1}{2} = \frac{9}{2}$$ The fraction is now $$2 + \cfrac{1}{1 + \cfrac{1}{1 + \cfrac{1}{\frac{9}{2}}}}$$

$$\frac{1}{\frac{9}{2}} = \frac{2}{9}$$

$$1 + \frac{2}{9} = \frac{11}{9}$$ Now we have $$2 + \cfrac{1}{1 + \cfrac{1}{\frac{11}{9}}}$$

$$\frac{1}{\frac{11}{9}} = \frac{9}{11}$$

$$1 + \frac{9}{11} = \frac{20}{11}$$ So now we have $$2 + \cfrac{1}{\frac{20}{11}}$$

Finally, we get $$2 + \frac{11}{20} = \frac{51}{20}$$

Here's a listing of a computer program which combines these two algorithms, followed by a run using 2.55 as input.

CONTINUED
FRACTIONS

```
LIST
10 DIM R(20)
20 A$="###.############"
30 B$="    ############"
40 PRINT
50 PRINT "THIS PROGRAM CONVERTS DECIMALS TO FRACTIONS."
60 PRINT
80 INPUT Y
90 PRINT "HOW MANY LEVELS (1 TO 12)?"
100 INPUT T
110 PRINT
120 FOR A=1 TO T
130 R(A)=INT(Y+.00001)
140 IF ABS(R(A)-Y)<.00001 THEN 180
150 Y=1/(Y-R(A))
160 NEXT A
170 GOTO 190
180 T=A
190 PRINT R(1);" +  1"
```

HERE'S WHERE THE FORMATS USED IN LINES 330, 350, AND 360 ARE DEFINED.

```
200  FOR A=2 TO T-1
210  PRINT TAB(A*6-7);"---------"
220  PRINT TAB(A*6-6);R(A);"  +   1"
230  NEXT A
240  PRINT TAB(T*6-7);"-----"
250  PRINT TAB(T*6-6);R(T)
260  N=R(T)
270  D=1
280  FOR B=T-1 TO 1 STEP -1
290  A=N
300  N=R(B)*N+D
310  D=A
320  NEXT B
330  PRINT USING B$,N
340  PRINT "=   ------------- = ";
350  PRINT USING A$,N/D
360  PRINT USING B$,D
370  END
```

```
RUN


THIS PROGRAM CONVERTS DECIMALS TO FRACTIONS.

? 2.55
HOW MANY LEVELS (1 TO 12)?
? 12

  2   +   1
        ---------
          1   +   1
                ---------
                  1   +   1
                        ---------
                          4   +   1
                                -----
                                  2

                51
=  ------------- =    2.550000000000
                20
```

Here's a run of this same program on a system with a BASIC that has "multiple-precision floating point arithmetic". Up to 15 decimal digits of accuracy can be handled by this system, which is why we used fifteen # symbols in defining A$:

A$ ="###.############"

Since we allowed for three digits in front of the decimal, this leaves room for twelve digits after the decimal. As you can see, our final fraction was equal to the decimal

3.141592653580

which agrees with the input decimal's 12 significant digits. Since different versions of BASIC have different "precisions" of arithmetic, you may not obtain exactly the same results.

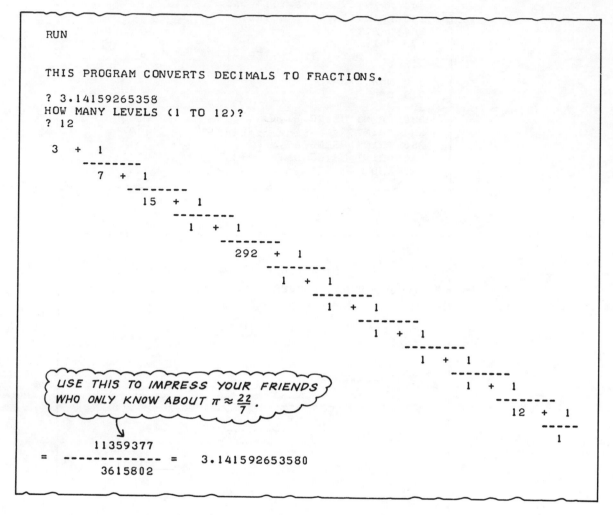

3.8 SAVING YOUR PROGRAMS

Now that your programs are getting a bit lengthy, you will be looking for some method of storing them outside the computer's memory for later use. Three kinds of "external" storage are usually used: punched paper tape, magnetic disk, and magnetic tape (usually in the form of cassettes or cartridges).

Saving Programs on Paper Tape

Until lately a widespread (and cheap) way of storing programs externally was on punched paper tape. The popularity of this method was due to the use of terminals in schools and industry which had a paper tape punch and paper tape reader built in. Here's what the usual 8-channel paper tape looks like:

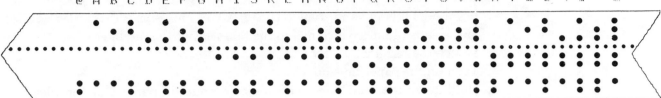

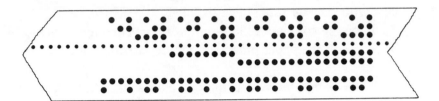

NOTE: The lower tape is spaced normally. The upper tape has "null" (no punch) typed in between each character. The ASCII (American Standard Code for Information Interchange) meaning of the punched codes is shown above it. A chart of all these codes is given in Appendix B.

Paper tape has eight positions for holes but only seven are used for the bits of the ASCII code. For example, for the letter L the ASCII code is

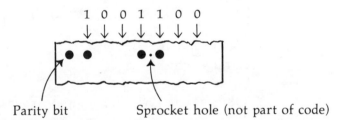

Parity bit   Sprocket hole (not part of code)

The eighth punched hole (at the left) is called a "parity bit" and it's used to make the total number of bits even for error checking (if the computer doesn't find an *even* number of bits "on", there's an error).

Punching a paper tape copy of a program is only a little more complicated than getting a listing. The main thing to keep in mind is that when you later read the tape back in, the computer will react just as if someone were typing the program into the terminal. So you should be careful when you turn on the paper tape punch that whatever gets punched will be acceptable when it is later read back in. That's the reasoning behind the following steps:

1. Make sure the program you want to save is in memory. If your BASIC has a NULL command, type NULL 3 (CR) (This puts 3 extra blank codes at the ends of lines which makes the tapes easier to read later on.)
2. Switch the terminal to "local".
3. Turn on the paper tape punch.
4. Hold down the "null" key to get a blank length of paper tape for a leader. (On some terminals, a different key may have to be used, e.g., "here is").
5. Turn *off* the paper tape punch.
6. Switch the terminal back to "line".
7. Type the command LIST—*do not type carriage return.*
8. Turn *on* the paper punch; *now type carriage return*

The computer will print out a listing, and it will be recorded on the paper tape. When the listing and punching is finished,

9. Switch the terminal to "local".
10. Hold down the "null" key to get a blank length of tape for a tail.
11. Turn *off* the paper tape punch.
12. Detach the paper tape, roll it up before it gets stepped on, label the leader with the program name and date (it helps to know when to throw it out). Rubberband it. (Adhesive type tape will get gummy on oiled paper tape in time.)

What you have actually recorded on punched tape is:

carriage return,
line feed,
your program,
carriage return,
line feed,
'OK' (or whatever your computer says when it completes a LIST).

Loading Programs from Paper Tape

Reading in the paper tape should be thought of like typing in a program. Start by doing whatever your computer requires before typing in a NEW program, then:

1. Insert your paper tape in the reader.
2. Turn on the reader, and sit back and watch.
3. Remove tape when finished, roll it up again before it gets stepped on. Turn off reader.

Ignore the error message that may be triggered by the 'OK' (or whatever) that was recorded on the tape.

4. To see what got read in, type LIST.
5. Examine the listing for obvious mistakes—paper tape readers have been known to lose a bit here and there.
6. Make corrections in exactly the same manner as you would for a program that had just been typed in.

In spite of the problems noted above, paper tape does provide a reasonably reliable method of storing programs. Even if you have magnetic storage, paper tape provides a good backup.

Saving Program Output on Punched Paper Tape

For those who have the paper tape reader-punch on their terminal, the following trick is possible. When you need several copies of the same output (to give to friends or decorate your wall, etc.) copy it onto punched tape. Then, instead of recomputing this output, just read the tape with the terminal on "local".

Saving and Loading Programs on Disk

If paper tape is the least sophisticated way of getting data in and out of a computer, magnetic disk is the most sophisticated. There are a number of systems on the market which use a disk to save both programs and data. The procedure described here is for an Altair with one floppy disk drive.

In addition to physically inserting and removing the disk, you must "logically" connect and disconnect it using the commands MOUNT and UNLOAD (not DISMOUNT as you might expect). This lets your computer system know that the disk is there and allows it to do all the preliminary operations that make data transfer so simple. After inserting the disk, you type:

MOUNT 0   (This command is *not* needed on the TRS–80 or Apple II)

(Zero is the number of the first disk drive. If you only have one, it's zero.)
Before removing the disk at the end of a session, you type:

UNLOAD 0   (This command is *not* needed on the TRS-80 or Apple II)

After a disk has been mounted, you can save a program you have written by simply typing

SAVE "DIET4"   (On the Apple II use SAVE DIET4)

where DIET4 is the name under which you "file" the program. The computer then takes care of finding a free space on the disk and storing your program in it. Rules for naming files on this system are: (1) it must be one to eight characters long, and (2) there can be no numbers or special characters as the first character.

To see what programs (or data files) you have saved, type:

FILES   (or CATALOG or CAT or DIR)

The computer will print out all the names of files on the disk currently in the disk drive. A program already saved on disk is loaded into memory by typing:

LOAD "DIET4"   or   RUN "DIET4"

In both cases the disk is searched for the file you name, memory is erased and the file DIET4 is loaded into memory. In the second case, it is also immediately run.

If you decide to change the name of a stored file, type:

NAME "DIET4" AS "DIET2"

You can get rid of a stored file by simply typing:

KILL "DIET2"

Some of the above commands (not MOUNT or UNLOAD) can be used within a program. Read the reference manual for your computer before trying any file commands.

Saving and Loading Programs on Cassette Tape

Cassette storage systems are at a level of sophistication in between punched paper tape and disk. They are faster than most paper tape systems but slower and less flexible than disk. Here is a procedure on an Altair cassette system for saving a file you name "HAROLD":

1. Turn on the tape recorder and position the tape cassette to a free space.
2. Type CSAVE "HAROLD", *do not type carriage return.*
3. Start the tape recorder recording. *Type carriage return.*
   Only the first character of HAROLD is used as the label of the saved file.
4. When the computer prints OK, turn off the tape recorder.
5. Write the file name and date on the cassette label.

To load files from cassette:

1. Turn on the recorder, insert the cassette and rewind it.
2. Type CLOAD "HAROLD", *do not type carriage return.*
3. Press "play". *Type carriage return.*
4. When the computer prints OK, turn off the recorder.

The computer will clear memory, search the cassette tape until it finds the file name HAROLD (just the first character) and load it into memory. If this doesn't work don't be surprised—cassette storage is sometimes erratic. Try again.

3.9   PROJECT IDEAS

1. Write a program to print Pascal's triangle. This is a triangular pattern of numbers which has 1's along the edges. All the other numbers have the property that they equal the sum of the two numbers just above them in the pattern. It also turns out that the numbers across row K give the combinations of K things taken 0 at a time, 1 at a time, etc. For example, row 5 has the numbers 1,5,10,10,5,1. If you think of these as giving how many "combination sandwiches" are possible, first from 5 ingredients taken 0 at a time (the null sandwich), then 1 at a time, 2 at a time, etc., you see that the total number of combinations is 1+5+10+10+1=32. Now go back and look at the hot dog problem in Section 2.4 and you'll see that we have discovered a new way of solving the same problem. It's a small world.

   Here's what a run of your program should look like:

```
RUN

HOW MANY LEVELS (MAX.= 12)? 12
                                   1

                                1     1

                             1     2     1

                          1     3     3     1

                       1     4     6     4     1

                    1     5    10    10     5     1

                 1     6    15    20    15     6     1

              1     7    21    35    35    21     7     1

           1     8    28    56    70    56    28     8     1

        1     9    36    84   126   126    84    36     9     1

     1    10    45   120   210   252   210   120    45    10     1

  1    11    55   165   330   462   462   330   165    55    11     1

1    12    66   220   495   792   924   792   495   220    66    12     1
```

2. One of the difficulties with making graphs on an alphanumeric terminal is that you can't always put the plotting characters exactly where they belong. Sometimes it's better to leave out characters that would plot in "bad" positions, and let the viewer mentally fill in what's missing. Write a program that does this for a circle, with an output that "suggests" a perfect circle. The equation for a circle of radius R is:

Y= SQR(R*R-X*X)

Since the SQR function only gives + values, you'll have to take care of also plotting the - values. Here's an example of what the output might look like.

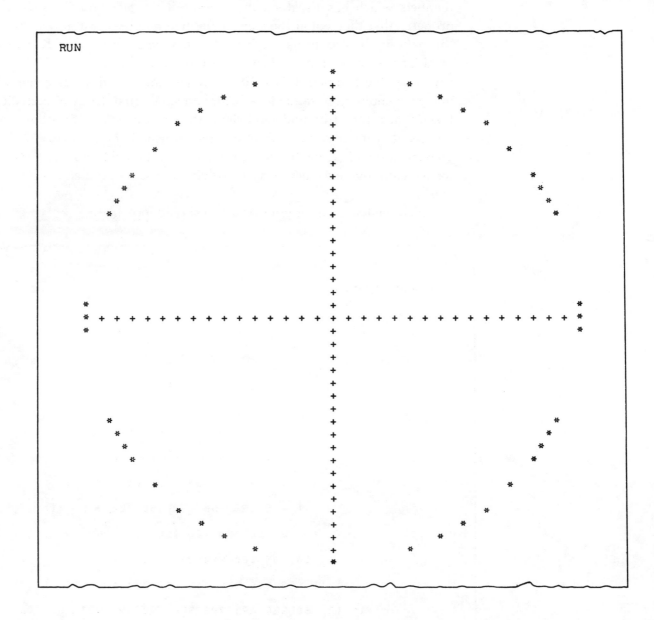

3. Rewrite one of the programs from this chapter in minimal BASIC, using remarks and indentations to clarify the program's structure. An example showing some techniques that can be used is given below. On some computers you use a colon to get blank lines (e.g., 105:)

THE STYLE
CORNER

```
100 REM     WATCHER     28 SEPTEMBER 1977     JOHN M. NEVISON
105
110 REM     THIS PROGRAM IS A STYLED VERSION OF AN ORIGINAL
115 REM     PROGRAM BY T. DWYER AND M. CRITCHFIELD.
120
125 REM     REFERENCE:  DWYER, T. AND CRITCHFIELD, M., "BASIC AND
130 REM                 THE PERSONAL COMPUTER," READING, MASS:
135 REM                 ADDISON-WESLEY PUBLISHING COMPANY, 1978.
140
145 REM     PRINT A TABLE AND A GRAPH OF A WEIGHT-WATCHER'S
150 REM     PROGRESS.  PRINT A CUSTOMIZED GRAPH IF ONE
155 REM     IS REQUESTED.
160
165 REM     VARIABLES:
170 REM          A.....LOW END OF THE GRAPH
175 REM          B.....HIGH END OF THE GRAPH
180 REM          A$....ANSWER TO A QUESTION
185 REM          D.....DIFFERENCE BETWEEN TWO WEIGHTS
190 REM          I.....INDEX VARIABLE
195 REM          S.....SUM OF THE WEIGHT LOST
200 REM          W.....PREVIOUS WEEK'S WEIGHT
205 REM          X.....INTERVAL COUNTER
210
215 REM     CONSTANTS:
220         LET G9 = 122                      'THE GOAL WEIGHT
225         LET N9 = 12                       'THE NUMBER OF WEEKS DONE
230         DIM W(12)
235         FOR I = 1 TO N9
240             READ W(I)                     'THE WEEKLY WEIGHTS
245         NEXT I
250         DATA 153, 149.5, 147.5, 147.5, 145, 144.5, 141, 141.5, 139.25
255         DATA 139.5, 137.5, 138.5
260
265
270 REM     MAIN PROGRAM
275
280         GO SUB 390                        'PRINT TABLE
285         LET A = 100
290         LET B = 200
295         GO SUB 520                        'PRINT GRAPH
300
305         PRINT
310         PRINT "WANT A CUSTOMIZED GRAPH";
315         INPUT A$                          '*
320         IF A$ <>  "YES" THEN 370
325             PRINT "WHAT IS THE SMALLEST NUMBER THAT ";
330             PRINT "YOU WANT (INSTEAD OF 100)";
335             INPUT A
340             PRINT "WHAT IS THE LARGEST NUMBER THAT ";
345             PRINT "YOU WANT (INSTEAD OF 200)";
350             INPUT B
355             GO SUB 520                    'PRINT GRAPH
360             PRINT "WANT ANOTHER GRAPH";
365         GO TO 315                         '*
370
375         STOP
380
385
```

```
390 REM     SUBROUTINE:  PRINT TABLE
395 REM       IN:  G, W()
400 REM       OUT:
405
410     PRINT "WEIGHT WATCHER'S RECORD"
415     PRINT
420     PRINT "WEEK", "WEIGHT", "DIFFERENCE"
425     LET S = O
430
435     PRINT 1, W(1), O
440     LET W = W(1)
445     FOR I = 2 TO N9
450        LET D = W(I) - W
455        LET S = S + D
460        PRINT I, W(I), D
465        LET W = W(I)
470     NEXT I
475
480     PRINT
485     PRINT "AVG. WEEKLY LOSS  "; S/ I    ; "POUNDS"
490     PRINT "POUNDS TO GOAL   "; W-G9
495     PRINT "TOTAL POUNDS LOST SO FAR  "; S
500     PRINT
505
510 RETURN
515
520 REM     SUBROUTINE:  PRINT GRAPH
525 REM       IN:   A, B, W()
530 REM       OUT:
535
540 REM     PRINT THE HEADING LINE 1, THE HEADING LINE 2,
545 REM     AND THE LINES OF THE GRAPH.
550
555     PRINT "WEIGHT WATCHER'S GRAPH"
560     PRINT
565
570     LET X = O
575
580
585     FOR I = A TO B STEP 10
590        PRINT TAB(X*50* (10/(B-A)) + 5); I;
595        LET X = X + 1
600     NEXT I
605     PRINT
610
615     PRINT "    I"
620     FOR I = 1 TO (X-1)
625        PRINT TAB(I*50* (10/(B-A)) + 7); "*";
630     NEXT I
635     PRINT
640
645     FOR I = 1 TO N9
650        PRINT I; TAB(4); "I"; TAB((W(I)-A) *(50/(B-A)) + 6); "+"
655     NEXT I
660
665 RETURN
670
675     END
```

```
100 REM            CHAPTER 3, PROJECT IDEA #4
105 REM
110 REM            WRITE A PROGRAM THAT CONSISTS ENTIRE-
120 REM            LY OF REMARK STATEMENTS AT FIRST.
125 REM
130 REM            THEN EXPAND THE REMARK IDEAS
140 REM            INTO BLOCKS OF EXECUTABLE STATEMENTS
155 REM
160 REM                       EXAMPLE
170 REM
199 REM-------------------------------------
200 REM    BLOCK 200 STATEMENTS ARE TO READ
201 REM    IN WEEKLY STOCK PRICES OVER YEAR
299 REM-------------------------------------
300 REM    BLOCK 300 STATEMENTS ARE TO PRINT
301 REM    A TABLE OF PRICES FOR EACH WEEK
399 REM-------------------------------------
400 REM    BLOCK 400 WILL FIND MAX AND MIN PRICES
499 REM-------------------------------------
500 REM    BLOCK 500 WILL ASK THE USER HOW MANY
501 REM    COLUMNS ARE AVAILABLE FOR A GRAPH
502 REM    AND THEN CALCULATE SCALE FACTORS
599 REM-------------------------------------
600 REM    BLOCK 600 WILL MAKE A GRAPH OF PRICES
699 REM-------------------------------------
999 END
```

20 PRINT "MARY"

90 PRINT X

10 FOR I = 1 TO 100 STEP 2

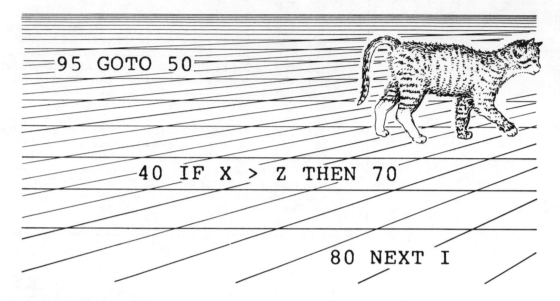

95 GOTO 50

40 IF X > Z THEN 70

80 NEXT I

4
A BIT OF
ADVANCED BASIC

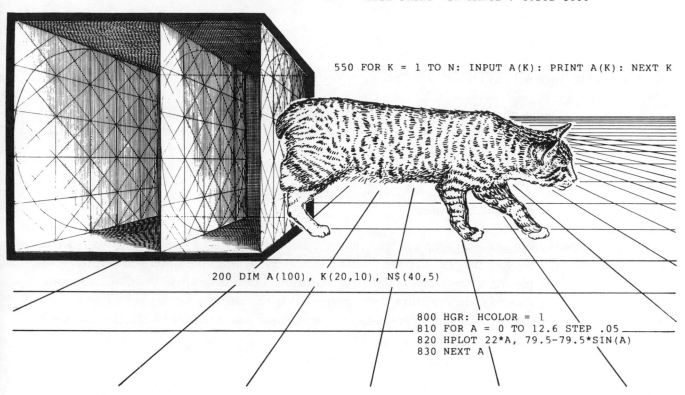

```
430 FOR F = 1 TO 3: PRINT TAB(13*(F-1));A$(P(R),F);: NEXT F: PRINT
```

```
320 IF NOT(A>X OR B<Y) THEN PRINT "OUT OF RANGE": GOSUB 2500
                       ELSE PRINT "IN RANGE": GOSUB 3500
```

```
550 FOR K = 1 TO N: INPUT A(K): PRINT A(K): NEXT K
```

```
200 DIM A(100), K(20,10), N$(40,5)
```

```
800 HGR: HCOLOR = 1
810 FOR A = 0 TO 12.6 STEP .05
820 HPLOT 22*A, 79.5-79.5*SIN(A)
830 NEXT A
```

4.0 INTRODUCTION

The features of BASIC covered in the first three chapters allow one to write programs for a large variety of applications, including some that are quite complex. In particular, just about any "number crunching" program (one that uses arithmetic operations to manipulate numerical data) can be written in minimal BASIC. However such programs can become very long, and difficult to understand. One soon gets the idea that it would be valuable to have additional BASIC statements that express complex ideas in a more structured form.

Another limitation of minimal BASIC is that it doesn't allow you to manipulate text (such as words, sentences, or paragraphs) with the same ease as numbers. A third problem is that minimal BASIC (like most other professional computer languages) was not designed to handle graphical output of the type now possible on video terminals and home color television sets.

To overcome these deficiencies, BASIC has been gradually expanded over the years, resulting in a version that is often called extended BASIC. Some of the best-known extended BASIC languages are BASIC-PLUS, Microsoft BASIC, TRS-80 Level II BASIC, PET BASIC, and APPLESOFT BASIC.

In this chapter we'll summarize the most important features of extended BASIC in section 4.1. Then in sections 4.2 and 4.3 we'll show you how to write two useful sorting programs that use some of these features. In section 4.4 we'll look at the special graphing features of Radio Shack TRS-80 Level II BASIC. Finally, in section 4.5, we'll explain how to use the high resolution color graphics features available on the Apple II computer.

4.1   AN OVERVIEW OF EXTENDED BASIC

A number of the features of extended BASIC were illustrated in project 4 at the end of section 2.9. In this section we'll explain these features in further detail, and describe several new ones.

Multiple Statements

One of the simplest features of extended BASIC to use when you wish to shorten programs is the *multiple statement*. A multiple statement is formed by placing several statements on the same line, separating them with colons. Another abbreviation that's permitted is to omit the keyword LET in assignment statements. For example, using these two features, the following three statements of minimal BASIC

```
10 LET X = 104.5
20 LET N = 10
30 LET Z9 = 35
```

can be written as the multiple statement

```
10 X = 104.5: N = 10:Z9 = 35
```

in extended BASIC. You can interpret the colon as the word "and", reading this statement as "LET X = 104.5 and LET N = 10 and LET Z9 = 35".

Use of the colon should not be overdone, otherwise programs become difficult to read. In particular, it's poor practice to use the colon to string statements together that have no logical connection. On the other hand, putting related statements on the same line can improve readability. For example, the following short FOR loop reads well as a multiple statement:

```
85 FOR J = 1 TO 10: B(J) = J*J: NEXT J
```

This statement stores the squares of the first ten integers in the B arrray, so after the statement is executed you'll have B(1) = 1, B(2) = 4, B(3) = 9, and so on up to B(10) = 100.

String Variables and String Arrays

The variable names we've seen so far (such as X, A, B(14), and N3) refer to locations in the computer's memory where numbers are stored. Strictly speaking they should be called "numeric variables".

To allow programmers to store non-numeric data—letters, words, sentences—extended BASIC also allows what are called *string variables*. These are indicated by adding a dollar sign to a letter. Examples are A$, B$, X$, and W$.

In computer programming, the word *string* means any sequence of characters. To show where the sequence starts and stops, quotation marks are used. Examples of strings are "BOB", "PLUTONIUM-88", "35 MAIN ST.", or even "##!!!@ A8!". Each of these is an example of a *string constant* that can be stored in a string variable.

To store a string constant in a string variable, you can use a LET statement like this:

```
20 LET A$ = "WHAMO"
```

Strings can also be stored by using READ and DATA statements as follows:

```
100 READ N$, M$
500 DATA "SUZIE", MIKE"
```

A third way to store strings in variables is to use the INPUT statement:

```
150 INPUT A$, B$, C$
```

For an example showing how to use the INPUT statement with string variables, re-study the program HI NAME of section 2.0.

The better extended BASIC languages also allow *string arrays*. These allow you to store a whole collection of strings in subscripted string variables such as A$(5), B$(20), or Z$(15). Here's an example showing how to use a string array called W$( ).

STRINGA

```
100 REM **************************************************
102 REM *      STRINGA (STRING ARRAY DEMONSTRATION)     #
105 REM **************************************************
110 DIM W$(21)
120 PRINT "AFTER EACH ? TYPE ONE WORD OF A SENTENCE."
130 PRINT "TYPE A PERIOD WHEN DONE.   LIMIT IS 20 WORDS."
140 REM ----- INPUT WORDS INTO STRING ARRAY -----
145 K=1
150 IF K>20 THEN 210
160   PRINT "WORD # "; K;
170   INPUT W$(K)
180   IF W$(K)= "." THEN 200
185   LET W$(K)=W$(K) + " "
190   K=K+1
195 GOTO 150
```

```
200 REM ----- PRINT WORDS IN REVERSE ORDER -----
210 PRINT: PRINT "HERE'S YOUR SENTENCE BACKWARDS:": PRINT
220 FOR J=K TO 1 STEP -1
230    PRINT W$(J);
240 NEXT J
250 PRINT: PRINT: PRINT "DONE"
260 END


RUN
AFTER EACH ? TYPE ONE WORD OF A SENTENCE.
TYPE A PERIOD WHEN DONE.  LIMIT IS 20 WORDS.
WORD #  1 ? DOCTOR
WORD #  2 ? LIVINGSTONE
WORD #  3 ? I
WORD #  4 ? PRESUME
WORD #  5 ? .

HERE'S YOUR SENTENCE BACKWARDS:

.PRESUME I LIVINGSTONE DOCTOR

DONE
```

A good way to understand how this program works is to visualize the string array as a block of memory locations organized as follows:

W$(1)	DOCTOR
W$(2)	LIVINGSTONE
W$(3)	I
W$(4)	PRESUME
W$(5)	.
W$(6)	
.	
.	
.	
W$(20)	

The first part of the program uses the subscripts $K = 1, 2, 3, 4, 5$ to store the words (strings) input by the user in the variables W$(K) in the order shown. Each string can be up to 255 characters long. The second part of the program then prints the words in the reverse order by using the subscript $J = 5, 4, 3, 2, 1$ to print the strings W$(J) from the same W$ array. This is the real power of string arrays; you can use a variable subscript to both store strings and to retrieve them.

A special string operator called concatenation (written as +) was used in line 185. This operator is used to put two strings together as a single string. For example, with concatenation "RAT" + "CAT" becomes "RATCAT". In our demonstration program we used concatenation in the form W$(K) + " " in order to add a space to each word. This was done so that the backward sentence would be printed with spaces between words.

Doubly Subscripted String Arrays

Double subscripts can be used on numeric variables to indicate the row and column in a *block* of variables. To see what this looks like, take another look at the last part of section 3.5 where we showed a diagram picturing a block of locations for the numeric array A(I,J). In that example, letting A(3,2) = 499 meant storing the number 499 in the third row and second column of the array A(I,J). In general, A(I,J) holds the data for the Ith row and Jth column of the array.

In a similar manner, you can store string data in a two-dimensional string array. For example, an array N$(I,J) might hold data as follows:

SMITH, JA	487-2906	CHEMIST
JONES, BE	382-1342	BIOLOGIST
ABLE, CB	563-4412	CHEF
FUERST, CJ	123-4567	PILOT

Each row in this array is used to hold related information about one person. The first column is used to hold the person's name, the second, the person's telephone number, and the third his or her occupation. In BASIC you can store this information in an array such as N$(I,J) by using LET statements, INPUT statements, or DATA statements. For example, LET N$(2,3) = "BIOLOGIST" would put the string "BIOLOGIST" in the second row, third column of N$(I,J). The same result can be had either by using the statement READ N$(2,3) combined with the statement DATA "BIOLOGIST", or by using INPUT N$(2,3) in the program, and then typing BIOLOGIST after the ? produced by the INPUT statement.

In most programs, a number of strings will have to be stored in memory, so instead of READ N$(2,3) or INPUT N$(2,3), the statement will more likely be READ N$(I,J) or INPUT N$(I,J). In this case I and J will be determined by two FOR loops used as shown in the program ARRAY DEMO 2 at the end of section 3.5. A complete example showing the use of string arrays for storing and sorting data will be given in section 4.3.

SELF-TEST

1. Write a program that uses a READ statement with DATA statements to fill in the entire string array shown above. (Hint: Use nested FOR loops). The program should then print the array in the reverse order, that is, print it as row 4, row 3, row 2, and row 1.
2. Re-write the program STRING ARRAY DEMO (the one that prints a sentence backwards) so that the input sentence is printed with alternate words reversed. For example, if you input FOR HE'S A JOLLY GOOD FELLOW., the program's output should be

HE'S FOR JOLLY A FELLOW GOOD.

The Extended IF statement

The IF statement can be extended in three ways. The first is to allow one or more statements after the word THEN (instead of a line number). Here are two examples:

```
15 IF X > 10 THEN LET Y = 5 * 10
25 IF E = 0 THEN PRINT "OUT OF ENERGY": LET E = 100: GOTO 99
30 PRINT "ENERGY NOT ZERO": GOTO 99
```

In the second example, the colon is used to link together three different statements which are to be executed when the conditon E = 0 is true. When the condition is false, *none* of these statements are executed; the program goes on to the next *numbered* statement (line 30 in our example).

The second extension of IF . . . THEN uses the word ELSE to show what should be done when a condition is *false*. Again, colons can be used to group several statements together.

```
350 IF X > 9 THEN PRINT "TOO LARGE": X = X −1
ELSE PRINT "RESULTS O.K.": S = S + X
```

The third extension is to allow several conditions to be used in the conditional part of the IF statement, provided they are joined by the "logical" connectives AND, OR, and NOT. For example,

```
150 IF X = 9 AND Y = 9 THEN 2000
```

This means that if *both* conditions are true then branch to line 2000.

```
60 IF E < 20 OR T > 99 THEN 3000
```

This means that if *either* condition is true then branch to line 3000.

70 IF NOT (X = 9 AND Y = 9) THEN 4000

This means that if it's *not* true that *both* X = 9 and Y = 9, then branch to line 4000.

What To Do If You Don't Have Extended BASIC

Many of the extended statements we've shown so far can be re-written in minimal BASIC by using several simpler statements. Here are some examples showing how the extended statements just shown can be translated back to minimal BASIC.

Most multiple statements can be translated into minimal BASIC by writing a new line for each colon (:). For example, the FOR loop

85 FOR J = 1 TO 10: B(J) = J * J: NEXT J

can be written as:

85 FOR J = 1 TO 10
86 B(J) = J * J
87 NEXT J

The IF . . . THEN followed by multiple statements (line 25 above) is a little trickier to translate.

25 IF E = 0 THEN 50
30 PRINT "ENERGY NOT ZERO"
35 GOTO 99
50 PRINT "OUT OF ENERGY"
55 LET E = 100
99 REM CONTINUE PROGRAM HERE

The IF . . . THEN . . . ELSE statement (line 350 above) gets translated in a similar manner:

350 IF X > 9 THEN 380
355 REM ELSE BLOCK
360 PRINT "RESULTS O.K."
365 LET X = S + X
370 GOTO 400
375 '
380 REM THEN BLOCK
385 PRINT "TOO LARGE"
390 LET X = X = 1
400 REM CONTINUE PROGRAM

The apostrophe used in 375' is a shorthand for REM allowed in some BASICs. We used it just to space things out for readability. You can also use 375 REM, or just omit this line.

Here's how the AND connective (line 150) is translated:

```
150 IF X = 9 THEN 170
160 GOTO 180
170 IF Y = 9 THEN 2000
180 REM AT LEAST ONE CONDITION NOT TRUE IF AT THIS LINE (etc.)
2000 REM BOTH CONDITIONS TRUE IF AT THIS LINE (etc.)
```

The OR condition (line 60) is translated as follows:

```
60 IF E < 20 THEN 3000
65 IF T > 99 THEN 3000
```

The logical NOT can be eliminated by using the complementary condition.

```
NOT X = 9    becomes    X < > 9
NOT X < 9    becomes    X > = 9
NOT X > 9    becomes    X < = 9
```

and so on. When NOT modifies a group of conditions then some laws of logic (De Morgan's laws) tell us that we must use the complementary conditions and *also* interchange AND with OR (and vice versa). So

```
70 IF NOT (X = 9 AND Y = 9) THEN 4000
```

should be rewritten as

```
70 IF X < > 9 OR Y < > 9 THEN 4000
```

This can then be written in minimal BASIC as

```
70 IF X < > 9 THEN 4000
71 IF Y < > 9 THEN 4000
```

Other Features of Extended BASIC

There are quite a few other features of extended BASIC, and new ones are being added each year. These include a variety of string functions, special input and output statements for dealing with "joystick" control, and an extensive set of disk file statements. Further information on these statements and examples of the use of all the features of extended BASIC can be found in *BASIC and the Personal Computer* (Addison-Wesley, Reading, Mass. 01867).

4.2   USING EXTENDED BASIC: INSERTION SORT

An algorithm is like a recipe. It gives a set of exact instructions on how to take input "ingredients", and transform them into something different (the output).

To be more precise, an algorithm is "a finite set of rules which gives a sequence of operations for solving a problem". Algorithms have five properties:

(1)   They must stop after a *finite* number of steps.
(2)   Each step must be *unambiguous*, that is, have only one meaning.
(3)   Algorithms accept zero or more *inputs*.
(4)   Algorithms produce one or more *outputs*.
(5)   They are *effective*, that is, each step can be done on a finite machine in a finite time.

To satisfy property (2), algorithms have to be expressed in unambiguous languages like BASIC. Correct BASIC programs are really algorithms expressed in a special form.

An important class of algorithms used in computing has to do with the problem of sorting. *Sorting* is the process of putting a list of things in order. The list may contain numbers, and look like this:

INPUT: 2.34, 7.8, -2, 3.2

Sorted in increasing order, this list becomes:

OUTPUT: -2, 2.34, 3.2, 7.8

We can also sort alphabetic data, like this:

INPUT: Zeke, Abe, Sally, Charlie

Sorted alphabetically, this list becomes:

OUTPUT: Abe, Charlie, Sally, Zeke

There are many algorithms for sorting. Most of them depend on *comparing* items in the list and then *swapping* pairs of items. This process must be repeated many times to sort a large list. This means sorting can take lots of computer time. Let's look at the problem more closely.

Insertion Sort

In this section we'll study the insertion sort algorithm, so called because it is similar to the sorting procedure used by card players when they insert new cards into a hand of cards. It is a very efficient algorithm for sorting small batches of items—up to about 100. However, every time you double the number of items to be sorted, the time required to do the sorting could increase by about a factor of four.* So if sorting 50 items takes 10 seconds, sorting 100 items will take about 40 seconds, 200 items will take about 160 seconds, 400 items, 640 seconds, and so on. When there are hundreds (or even thousands) of items to be sorted, other algorithms are usually preferred. Two of these (Shell Sort and Quicksort) are referenced in the exercises.

We'll first describe insertion sort in general terms, and then show how the algorithm translates into BASIC. Imagine that you have a hand of cards labeled with the values shown, and that at the present time they are organized as follows:

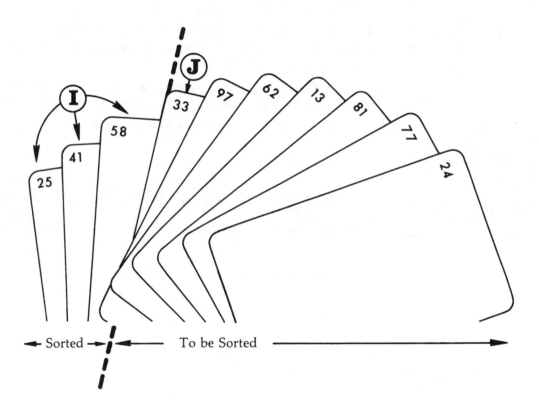

Our picture shows the hand at a time when it has been partially sorted.

The goal is to successively take cards from the right side starting at position J, and insert each one into it's proper place on the left side. In our example, we want the cards to eventually be ordered 13, 24, 25, 33, 41, 58, 62, 77, 81, 97.

To see how to proceed, assume that you have reached the point shown where the three cards to the left of the dashed line are already properly ordered.

---

*This rule assumes that the items are randomly ordered before sorting (see the SELF-TEST questions at the end of this section for more on this).

We'll use the variable J as a *pointer* to the position at the right of this dashed line. Our picture is shown after some sorting has already taken place, and J = 4.

The variable I is used to "point" at successive cards to the left of this boundary (for I = 3, 2, 1). The card at J will then be compared with each of these cards. When we find a card at position I such that the card at J is greater than or equal to the card at I, we will insert card J just to the right of card I. For the cards in our picture here's what will happen:

```
      For J = 4, CARD(J) = 33
Now   LET I = 3. Is CARD(J) > = CARD(I)? No.
      LET I = 2. Is CARD(J) > = CARD(I)? No.
      LET I = 1. Is CARD(J) > = CARD(I)? Yes.
```

Therefore we will insert CARD(J) to the right of CARD(I). This puts CARD(4) just to the right of CARD(1).

To make this algorithm work in BASIC we'll store the unsorted card numbers in an array with elements called R(1), R(2), R(3), . . . , R(N). We'll start with the dashed line to the right of the first card, so J = 2 at the beginning. Then for J = 2, 3, 4, . . . , N we'll apply the insertion algorithm just described.

One question that will arise is "How do you insert into an already filled array?" The trick we'll use is to first store the card number at J in a temporary variable by writing T = R(J). Then each time we *don't* do an insertion, we'll move a card number over to the right by using the statement R(I + 1) = R(I). That way we'll be making room for the eventual insertion of the Jth card when we write R(I + 1) = T.

Here's a BASIC program that employs this algorithm. It starts by using the random number generator in line 20 to fill up the R( ) array. The insertion sort then takes place in lines 30 to 130. The sorted numbers are printed in line 190.

INSERT

```
4 REM *************************************************
5 REM *    INSERT (INSERTION SORT USING RANDOM NUMBERS)    *
6 REM *************************************************
9 DIM R(160)
10 PRINT "HOW MANY NOS. TO BE SORTED";: INPUT N
12 IF N<1 OR N>160 PRINT "MIN IS 1, MAX IS 160":GOTO 10
13 :
14 REM ----- PUT RANDOM NUMBERS IN R( ) AND PRINT THEM -----
15 FOR K=1 TO N: R(K)=RND(0): NEXT K: REM--USE RND(1) ON APPLE
20 PRINT "NUMBERS TO BE SORTED ARE:": GOSUB 910: PRINT
22 :
23 REM ----- START THE MAIN LOOP OF THE INSERTION SORT -----
25 IF N=1 THEN 180
30 FOR J=2 TO N
70     I=J-1: T=R(J)
75     REM ----- START OF I LOOP FOR INSERTION -----
80     IF I<=0 THEN 120
```

```
85       IF T>=R(I) THEN 120
90          R(I+1)=R(I)
100         I=I-1
110         GOTO 80
120      REM ----- END OF I LOOP FOR INSERTION -----
125      R(I+1)=T
130 NEXT J
140 REM ----- END OF THE MAIN LOOP FOR INSERTION SORT -----
150 :
170 REM ----- NOW PRINT THE SORTED NUMBERS -----
180 PRINT ">>>>>>>>>  SORTED NUMBERS ARE >>>>>>>>>"
190 GOSUB 900
200 END
210 REM =======================================================
900 REM ----- SUBROUTINE TO PRINT IN 3 COLUMNS OF WIDTH 13 ----
910 FOR K= 1 TO N
920     T=K-3*INT((K-1)/3)
930     PRINT TAB(13*(T-1)); R(K);
940     IF T>=3 THEN PRINT
950 NEXT K
990 RETURN
RUN
HOW MANY NOS. TO BE SORTED? 11
NUMBERS TO BE SORTED ARE:
 .888076       .787762       .862675
 .735285       .476059       .55141
 .245708       .242171       .968336
 .721014       .592453
>>>>>>>>>  SORTED NUMBERS ARE >>>>>>>>>
 .242171       .245708       .476059
 .55141        .592453       .721014
 .735285       .787762       .862675
 .888076       .968336
```

SELF-TEST

1. Run the program INSERT for values of N = 20, 40, 80, and 160. Use a watch to time each run, and see if the ratio of successive times approaches the theoretical 4 to 1 ratio.

2. Modify INSERT so that the numbers to be sorted are *already* in order (Hint: Change R(K) = RND(0) in line 20 to R(K) = K). Now compare the times for N = 20, 40, 80, and 160. Are the ratios of successive times still four to one? In other words, is insertion sort "smart enough" not to waste a lot of time sorting numbers that are already in order?

3. Repeat question 2 for data that is *almost* in order (which is the case, for example, when only a few new items are added to an already sorted list).

4. If a large number of items need to be sorted, algorithms with better performance should be used. Two of the best are Shell Sort and Quicksort. These are explained in chapter 5 of *BASIC and the Personal Computer* (Addison-Wesley, 1978). Write a Shell Sort program for your computer, and repeat the experiments in exercises 1, 2, and 3 above.

5. Repeat the experiments in exercises 1, 2, 3 above for a Quicksort program. Summarize your results for Insertion Sort, Shell Sort, and Quicksort in a table.

4.3   USING STRING ARRAYS AND POINTERS TO SORT BUSINESS RECORDS

Business data is often organized as a collection of *records*, where each record consists of several related pieces of information. These pieces are put in separate *fields* of the record. For example, records might be organized into three fields that contain a person's name, phone number, and occupation.

	Field 1	Field 2	Field 3
Record 1:	SMITH, JR	123-4896	ARCHITECT
Record 2:	JONES, AB	452-1234	PLUMBER

A good way to store such records is to use a two-dimensional string array. If the array is called A$(,) then the element A$(R,F) refers to the Rth row (record), and Fth column (field).

If we have a large collection of such records—say 100—and wish to retrieve information from this collection, then it would be valuable if we could print three sorted lists: one sorted by name, one sorted by phone number, and one sorted by occupation.

To do this we *could* use a sorting algorithm similar to the insertion sort described in the previous section. The problem is that moving all that string data around tends to slow down the algorithm considerably. To get around this problem, an elegant modification of the insertion sort can be employed. The idea is to set up a separate numeric *pointer* array P(I), and use it to tell us how to print the rows of A$(I,J) in proper order. For example, suppose the 7th record (row) should be listed in fourth place when doing an alphabetic ordering of occupations. Also suppose our program somehow or other made P(4) = 7. Then if we write

```
10 PRINT "THE FOURTH RECORD (ORDERED BY OCCUPATION) IS:"
20 FOR F = 1 TO 3
30 PRINT A$(P(4),F);
40 NEXT F
```

we'll see the computer print the *seventh* record. To make this work for a complete alphabetical listing, our program must adjust *all* the values in the P( ) array so they point out the correct ordering. Then we can use a FOR loop to print all the records (not just the fourth one) in proper order.

Here's a sorting program that is based on this idea. It first reads string data for the records from DATA statements into the array A$(,). It next asks you which field you want to use for sorting. A modified insertion sort is then used to adjust the values in the pointer array P( ), and the results are printed out in increasing order in lines 410 to 440.

The modification of the insertion sort consists in using the string data for *comparisons* but not for insertions. The comparison is written as:

IF A$(T,F) > = A$(P(I),F) THEN 380

However all the insertions are done in the pointer array P( ) with the statements

P(I + 1) = P(I)
and   P(I + 1) = T

This process will put exactly the right numbers in P( ), and we'll then be able to print the records in order, provided we print A$(P(R),F) instead of A$(R,F).

This is a rather advanced program, so don't be surprised if you have to do a lot of thinking and re-thinking to understand fully how it works. Here's the program with three sample runs:

INSERT 2

```
100 REM **********************************************************
101 REM * INSERT2 (INSERTION SORT OF RECORDS USING POINTERS) *
102 REM **********************************************************
105 PRINT "STAND BY FOR INITIALIZATION"
110 DIM A$(10,4), P(10)   :N=0
120 FOR R=1 TO 10
130   FOR F=1 TO 3
140   READ A$(R,F)
150   IF A$(R,F)="$" THEN 190
160   NEXT F
170   N=N+1
180 NEXT R
190 FOR I=1 TO N: P(I)=I: NEXT I
200 '-----------------------------------------------------
201 '      SELECT FIELD ON WHICH TO DO SORT
202 '-----------------------------------------------------
210 PRINT "SORT RECORDS USING WHICH FIELD (1,2,3)";: INPUT F
220 IF F<1 OR F>3 THEN 210
230 IF N=1 THEN 410
300 '-----------------------------------------------------
301 ' SORTING ROUTINE USING INSERTION SORT AND P() ARRAY
302 '-----------------------------------------------------
310 FOR J=2 TO N
320   I=J-1: T=P(J)
330   IF I<=0 THEN 380
340   IF A$(T,F) >= A$(P(I),F) THEN 380
350   P(I+1)=P(I)
360   I=I-1
370   GOTO 330
380   P(I+1)=T
```

```
390 NEXT J
400 '-----------------------------------------------------
401 '       PRINT RECORDS SORTED BY SPECIFIED FIELD
402 '-----------------------------------------------------
410 PRINT ">>>>> RECORDS SORTED ON FIELD #";F;" >>>>>":PRINT
420 FOR R=1 TO N
430   FOR F=1 TO 3: PRINT TAB(13*(F-1));A$(P(R),F);: NEXT F  : PRINT
440 NEXT R
999 STOP
1000 '----- STRING DATA FOR RECORDS -----
1001 DATA "SMITH, AB", "423-5436", "WRITER"
1002 DATA "EINSTEIN, A", "509-2541", "PATENT CLERK"
1003 DATA "SAWBONES, R", "976-2758", "SURGEON"
1004 DATA "BARON, RED", "708-1852", "PILOT"
1005 DATA "ATTILA, HN", "800-1234", "ADMINISTRATOR"
1999 DATA "$","$","$"
```

```
RUN
STAND BY FOR INITIALIZATION
SORT RECORDS USING WHICH FIELD (1,2,3)? 1
>>>>> RECORDS SORTED ON FIELD # 1  >>>>>


ATTILA, HN     800-1234      ADMINISTRATOR
BARON, RED     708-1852      PILOT
EINSTEIN, A    509-2541      PATENT CLERK
SAWBONES, R    976-2758      SURGEON
SMITH, AB      423-5436      WRITER




RUN
STAND BY FOR INITIALIZATION
SORT RECORDS USING WHICH FIELD (1,2,3)? 2
>>>>> RECORDS SORTED ON FIELD # 2  >>>>>


SMITH, AB      423-5436      WRITER
EINSTEIN, A    509-2541      PATENT CLERK
BARON, RED     708-1852      PILOT
ATTILA, HN     800-1234      ADMINISTRATOR
SAWBONES, R    976-2758      SURGEON




RUN
STAND BY FOR INITIALIZATION
SORT RECORDS USING WHICH FIELD (1,2,3)? 3
>>>>> RECORDS SORTED ON FIELD # 3  >>>>>


ATTILA, HN     800-1234      ADMINISTRATOR
EINSTEIN, A    509-2541      PATENT CLERK
BARON, RED     708-1852      PILOT
SAWBONES, R    976-2758      SURGEON
SMITH, AB      423-5436      WRITER
```

SELF-TEST

1. (Difficult) Modify the Shell Sort algorithm (explained in chapter 5 of *BASIC and the Personal Computer*) for use in sorting string records by means of a pointer array. The results should be the same as in the program INSERT 2 but the program should run more quickly when a large number of records are sorted (say 100 or more).

4.4 MEDIUM RESOLUTION GRAPHICS ON THE TRS-80

In chapter 3 we saw how to produce graphical output in BASIC by using the TAB(X) function. The plotting symbols used were alphanumeric characters such as "*" or "I". Since only a limited number of characters can be printed in a given space, these graphs are sometimes called "low-resolution".

On the TRS-80 computer there is an additional plotting feature available in the form of the BASIC statement SET(X,Y). When this statement is executed, it causes a small white rectangle to be printed on the output screen, X units to the right, and Y units down (positions are given with respect to the upper left-hand corner of the screen which is the position for X = 0 and Y = 0).

The rectangle is about one-fourth the size of a regular character. Rectangles can also be plotted in the spaces between lines, so graphs of finer resolution are possible. Overall, there are 128 plotting positions for X (numbered 0 to 127), and 48 plotting positions for Y (numbered 0 to 47). Thus a maximum of $128 \times 48 = 6,144$ rectangles can be plotted on the screen (as opposed to 1,024 characters).

Here's a simple TRS-80 Level II BASIC program that plots four lines in a tic-tac-toe pattern by using SET(X,Y) in four loops.

TICTAC

```
4 ´ *************************************************
5 ´ *        TICTAC (DEMO OF SET(X,Y) ON TRS-80)       *
6 ´ *************************************************
7 CLS
10 Y=15
20 FOR X=0 TO 127: SET(X,Y): NEXT X
30 Y=31
40 FOR X=0 TO 127: SET(X,Y): NEXT X
50 X=42
60 FOR Y=0 TO 47: SET(X,Y): NEXT Y
70 X=85
80 FOR Y=0 TO 47: SET(X,Y): NEXT Y
90 END
```

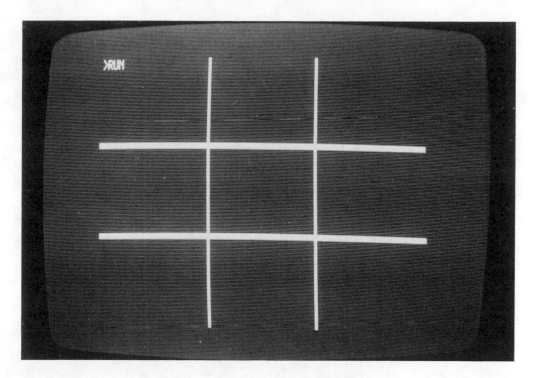

Run of TICTAC

When this program is run, the output will be as shown in the photograph. If you don't want the READY message to appear after the graph is finished, add the statement 85 GOTO 85. This freezes the picture by putting the computer in an infinite loop. To get out of this loop on the TRS-80 press BREAK (on other computers press CTRL and C simultaneously).

Graphs of mathematical functions can also be displayed with SET(X,Y), provided the graph is scaled to fit in the 128 by 48 grid pattern used by SET(X,Y). Here's an example showing the SIN (A) function plotted for A going from 0 to 12.7 radians (from 0 to about 720 degrees). Before studying the program, it would be a good idea to review the discussion of scaling in section 3.4. The scaling is done in lines 120 and 130 of this program. The scale factor in line 120 makes X go from 0 to 127. The scale factors in line 130 were chosen so that when SIN(A) goes from +1 to −1, Y goes from 0 to 47.

SETSINE

```
10 ´ ******************************************
11 ´ *      SETSINE  (TRS-80 SINE GRAPH)      *
12 ´ ******************************************
15 CLS
20 REM ..... DRAW VERTICAL AXIS WITH ´I´ .....
30 FOR V=1 TO 15: PRINT "I": NEXT V: PRINT "I";
35 ´
40 REM ..... DRAW HORIZONTAL AXIS WITH ´-´ .....
50 REM PRINT @ 0 MEANS PRINT AT THE BEGINNING OF THE FIRST LINE.
```

```
60 REM SINCE THERE ARE 64 CHARACTERS PER LINE, PRINT @ 64 MEANS
70 REM PRINT AT BEGINNING OF SECOND LINE, PRINT @ 128 MEANS PRINT
80 REM AT BEGINNING OF THIRD LINE, ETC.    TO PRINT HORIZONTAL AXIS
90 REM AT 8TH LINE WE THEREFORE USE PRINT @ 512 AS FOLLOWS:
100 PRINT @ 512, "%";
110 FOR H=1 TO 62: PRINT "-";: NEXT H
115 ´
120 REM ..... NOW DRAW SINE GRAPH USING SET(X,Y) .....
130 FOR A=0 TO 12.7 STEP .05
140    X=10*A
150    Y=47-23.5*(SIN(A)+1)
160    SET(X,Y)
170 NEXT A
180 PRINT @ 862, "PRESS BREAK TO EXIT";
190 GOTO 190
200 END
```

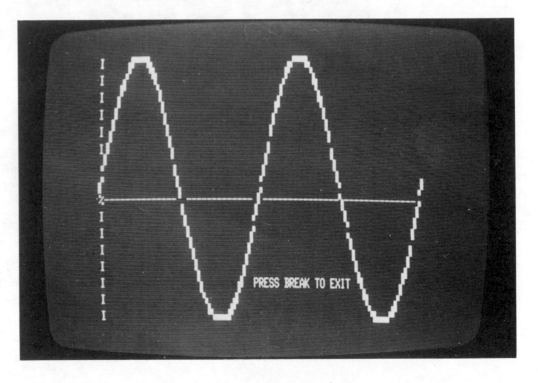

Run of SETSINE

An even fancier graph can be made by having both X and Y calculated as functions of A. The following program does this by using the SIN(2 * A) function for X, and the COS(3 * A) function for Y. The result is what physicists call a "2 by 3 Lissajous figure".

SETLISS

```
10 ' *********************************************
11 ' *       SETLISS  (TRS-80 LISSAJOUS FIGURE)      *
12 ' *********************************************
15 CLS
20 REM ..... DRAW VERTICAL AXIS WITH 'I' .....
30 FOR V=1 TO 15: PRINT TAB(31); "I": NEXT V: PRINT TAB(31); "I";
35 '
40 REM ..... DRAW HORIZONTAL AXIS WITH '-' .....
50 REM PRINT @ 0 MEANS PRINT AT THE BEGINNING OF THE FIRST LINE.
60 REM SINCE THERE ARE 64 CHARACTERS PER LINE, PRINT @ 64 MEANS
70 REM PRINT AT BEGINNING OF SECOND LINE, PRINT @ 128 MEANS PRINT
80 REM AT BEGINNING OF THIRD LINE, ETC.   TO PRINT HORIZONTAL AXIS
90 REM AT 8TH LINE WE THEREFORE USE PRINT @ 512 AS FOLLOWS:
100 PRINT @ 512, "";
110 FOR H=1 TO 62: PRINT "-";: NEXT H
115 '
120 REM ..... NOW DRAW LISSAJOUS FIGURE USING SET(X,Y) .....
130 FOR A=0 TO 6.3 STEP .025
140    X=63.5*SIN(2*A)+63.5
150    Y=23.5*COS(3*A)+23.5
160    SET(X,Y)
170 NEXT A
180 PRINT @ 862, "PRESS BREAK TO EXIT";
190 GOTO 190
200 END
```

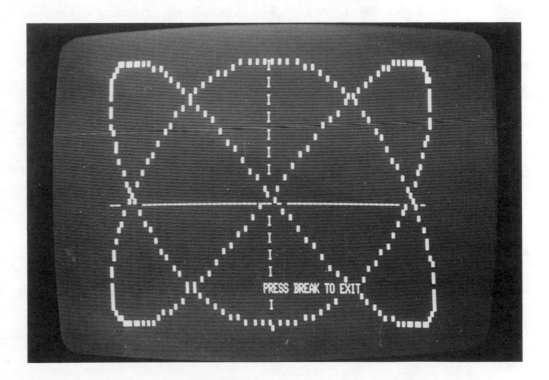

Run of SETLISS

4.5   COLOR GRAPHICS ON THE APPLE II

A number of microcomputers are able to display graphical output on a color TV set. One of the best-known of these is the Apple II computer. In this section we'll look at several programs written for this machine using the version of BASIC this company calls APPLESOFT BASIC.

The Apple II has two graphing modes. The first is called low resolution (LO RES for short) because it does its plotting with rectangular blocks on a 40 by 40 grid. Thus a total of 1600 rectangles can be placed on the screen. Each small rectangle is plotted by using the special BASIC statement PLOT X,Y where both X and Y must be integers between 0 and 39. For example, PLOT 10,20 would place a rectangle 10 units to the right, and 20 units down with respect to the upper left hand corner of the screen (which is position 0,0).

Before using PLOT X,Y this way, the Apple II must be put in LO RES graphing mode with the BASIC statement:

    100 GR

then the color must be set with a statement like this:

    110 COLOR = 2

There are 16 colors available corresponding to the numbers 0 to 15. Here's a program to draw 16 horizontal "dotted" lines, one for each color. You won't see the first line since the color 0 is "black".

LO RES DOTS

```
LIST
   10 REM   --- LO RES DOTS ---
   20 GR
   30 FOR N=0 TO 15
   40 COLOR=N
   50 Y=2*N+5
   60 FOR X=0 TO 38 STEP 2
   70 PLOT X,Y
   80 NEXT X
   90 NEXT N
  100 END
```

Run of LO RES DOTS

A graph of the sine function can also be plotted in LO RES mode. The low resolution graphics gives the output an interesting "chunky" appearance. Here's a listing and run of such a program. Lines 120 and 130 illustrate two additional LO RES graphics features used for plotting vertical lines and horizontal lines on the Apple II. The statement

    120 VLIN 0,39 AT 0

means draw a vertical line with Y going from 0 to 39, but with X fixed at 0. Similarly,

    240 HLIN 0,39 AT 19

means draw a horizontal line with X going from 0 to 39, but with Y fixed at 19. Line 155 of our program causes the colors to change from 1 to 13 as A goes from 0 to 12.6. Scale factors are used in lines 160 and 170 to make X and Y fit in the 40 by 40 grid.

LO RES SINE

```
LIST

10   REM  ---- LO RES SINE ----
100  GR
110  COLOR= 2
120  VLIN 0,39 AT 0
130  HLIN 0,39 AT 19
150  FOR A = 0 TO 12.6 STEP .05
155  COLOR= 1 + A
160  X = 3 * A
170  Y = 39 - 19.5 * ( SIN (A) + 1)
180  PLOT X,Y
190  NEXT A
```

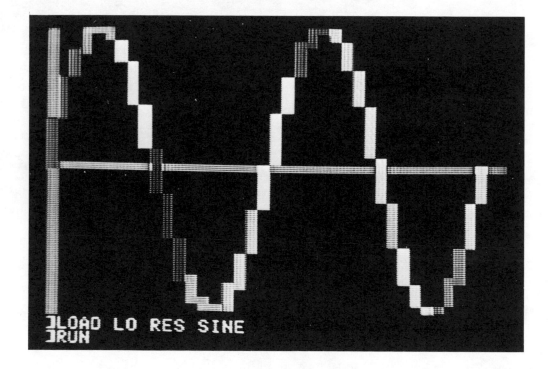

Run of LO RES SINE

High Resolution Apple Graphics

The Apple II computer has a second graphics mode called high resolution (HI RES for short) because it can plot a large number of very small rectangles on the TV screen. There are two BASIC statements that put the computer into HI RES mode. The first is

100 HGR

This statement switches the computer to a mode in which points can be plotted on a grid 280 units wide by 160 units high. Approximately one-sixth of the screen (at the bottom) is not used for graphing in this mode; it is reserved for printing ordinary characters. The BASIC statement

100 HGR2

puts the computer in a similar HI RES mode, except that this time the entire screen can be used for graphing. There is no room reserved at the bottom for characters, but the graphing grid is now 280 units wide by 192 units high.

Here's an Apple II program that plots the sine function using the first of these HI RES graphing modes. You'll notice that all the BASIC plotting words in HI RES mode start with the letter H. You should also know that eight codes are available in this mode for color, but two are "black" (HCOLOR = 0 and HCOLOR = 4). Also some colors don't work for some vertical lines!

Our program starts by using HCOLOR = 2 for plotting the axes. The axes are then drawn in lines 120 and 130. In HI RES mode there is only one BASIC plotting keyword (written HPLOT), but it can be used to plot lines as well as points. Line 130 plots a line from the point 0,0 to the point 0,159 for the vertical axis, while line 130 plots a line from the point 0,79) to 279,79 for the horizontal axis.

Next the color is set to 1 in line 140. Then the sine function is plotted with a FOR loop (lines 150 to 190). Scaled values of X and Y are calculated in lines 160 and 170, and each point X,Y is plotted in line 180. Line 175 is used to change the color of the graph when the angle A reaches 6.28 radians (360 degrees) just for fun.

HI RES SINE

```
     LIST
10   REM  ---- HI RES SINE ----
100    HGR
110    HCOLOR= 2
120    HPLOT 0,0 TO 0,159
130    HPLOT 0,79 TO 279,79
140    HCOLOR= 1
150    FOR A = 0 TO 12.6 STEP .05
160 X = 22 * A
170 Y = 159 - 79.5 * ( SIN (A) + 1)
175    IF A > 6.28 THEN  HCOLOR= 5
180    HPLOT X,Y
190    NEXT A
200    END
```

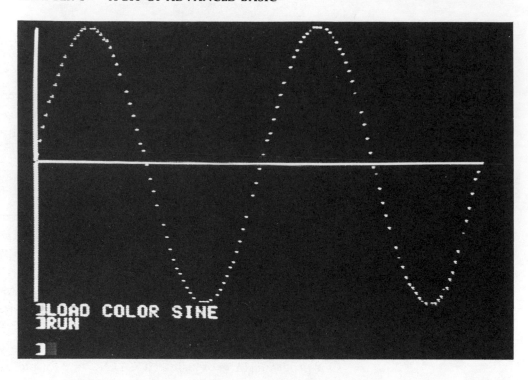

Run of HI RES SINE

As another illustration of how flexible the HPLOT statement is, here's a simple program that draws a sequence of line segments (also called *vectors*). The starting point is in the middle of the screen at 139,79. Each succeeding point is selected randomly and then a line is drawn from the old point to the new one. The overall effect is that of a random zig-zag pattern with the lines changing colors cyclically for C = 1 to 7. Since color 4 is black, there will be "breaks" in the pattern whenever C = 4.

RNDVECT

```
 LIST

5   REM  ---- RNDVECT ----
10  HGR :C = 1
20  X1 = 139:Y1 = 79
30  PRINT "HOW MANY VECTORS";: INPUT N
40  FOR I = 1 TO N
50  HCOLOR= C
60  X2 =   INT (280 *  RND (1)):Y2 =   INT (159 *  RND (1))
70  HPLOT X1,Y1 TO X2,Y2
80  X1 = X2:Y1 = Y2
90  C = C + 1
100  IF C > 7 THEN C = 1
110  NEXT I
120  PRINT "AGAIN (Y=YES)";: INPUT A$
130  IF A$ = "Y" THEN 10
140  END
```

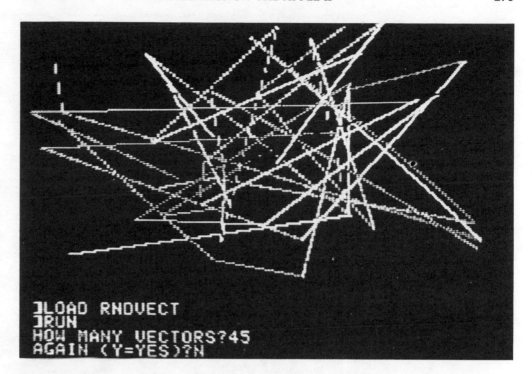

Run of RNDVECT

We'll conclude this section with two programs that use the HGR2 mode. The first one draws an artistic elliptical pattern. In lines 310 and 320 we make X2 and Y2 equal to scaled values of the SIN(A) and COS(A) functions. Analytic geometry tells us that therefore each of the points X2,Y2 must lie on an ellipse. We also randomly calculate points X1,Y1 near the center of this ellipse. Then in line 330 we plot line segments between these pairs of points, producing the result shown in the photograph. Of course the actual output will be in color, with the color of each line segment determined by the variable C.

ELLIPSE

```
      LIST

      10   REM   ---- ELLIPSE ----
      20   REM      PRESS CTRL AND C TO EXIT
      30 :
      100  HGR2
      110  HCOLOR= 7
      120  HPLOT 0,0 TO 279,0 TO 279,191 TO 0,191 TO 0,0
      130 :
      200  REM --- START PLOT LOOP ---
      205  HCOLOR= C
      210 X1 =  INT (100 *  RND (1) + 60)
      220 Y1 =  INT (80 *  RND (1) + 20)
      310 X2 = 130 *  SIN (A) + 138
      320 Y2 = 90 *  COS (A) + 95
```

```
330   HPLOT X1,Y1 TO X2,Y2
380 A = A + .1
385 C = C + 1
387   IF C > 7 THEN C = 0
390   GOTO 200
```

Run of ELLIPSE

Our last program works in a similar manner, except that X1 and Y1 are now fixed at the center, and X2 and Y2 describe a 3 × 2 Lissajous figure instead of an ellipse. The overall effect suggests an abstract painting of a butterfly.

LISSAJOUS

```
 LIST

10  REM        ----- LISSAJOUS -----
20  REM      PRESS CTRL AND C TO EXIT
30 :
100  HGR2
110  HCOLOR= 7
120  HPLOT 0,0 TO 279,0 TO 279,191 TO 0,191 TO 0,0
130 A = 0:C = 0
140 :
```

```
200   REM --- START PLOT LOOP ---
205   HCOLOR= C
210   X1 = 134
220   Y1 = 92
310   X2 = 130 *  SIN (2 * A) + 138
320   Y2 = 90 *  COS (3 * A) + 95
330   HPLOT X1,Y1 TO X2,Y2
380   A = A + .1
385   C = C + 1
387   IF C > 7 THEN C = 0
390   GOTO 200
```

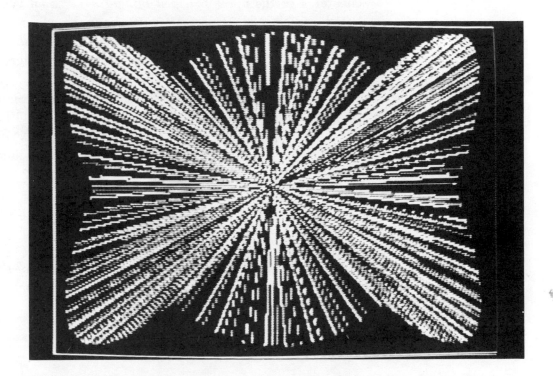

Run of LISSAJOUS

4.6   PROJECTS

1. Experiment with modifying the Lissajous programs (TRS-80 or Apple) by using SIN(M * A) and COS(N * A), where M and N are integers supplied by the user via the statement INPUT M,N placed at the beginning of the program. Which values of M and N give an ellipse? Which give a 3 × 2 Lissajous figure? How can you get a "figure eight" graph? What other values are interesting? What happens when M and N are switched?

2. Write a program that draws vectors (line segments) between points supplied by the user, and points randomly generated by the program or generated by mathematical functions. Investigate use of INKEY$ on the TRS-80 and GET on the Apple (or PET) as a means of obtaining user input.

3. (Advanced) Design a sequence of stick figure cartoons that successively move *parts* of the figure to give the illusion of motion. Then write a program to loop through this sequence over and over to produce a continuous "movie". Next try making the figure move across the screen while it simultaneously goes through its motions.

4. The extended string handling facilities of BASIC make it possible to write *word processing* programs. Investigate this subject, and see if you can write a simple text editing program. Information on how to do this can be found in chapter 4 of the book *You Just Bought a Personal What?* (BYTE Books, Peterborough, NH 03458). After you have the editor working, investigate the subject of a text formatter. An advanced discussion of a text formatter written in structured FORTRAN can be found in chapter 7 of *Software Tools* (Addison-Wesley, Reading MA 01867).

5. Write a program that uses the graphical output of a computer as both a display device and score keeper for the game of TIC TAC TOE. You'll want to extend the program TICTAC so that either a large "X" or large "O" can be drawn in the appropriate square. For example, if you number the squares 1, 2, 3 for the first row, 4, 5, 6 for the second row, and 7, 8, 9 for the last row, then the input:

Player X, WHAT IS YOUR MOVE? 5

should print a large "X" in the center square. The game should be played by two human players, but the computer should announce illegal moves, and also declare a winner.

APPENDIX A:
EXAMPLE OF USING TIMESHARING

Example of using a large timesharing system:

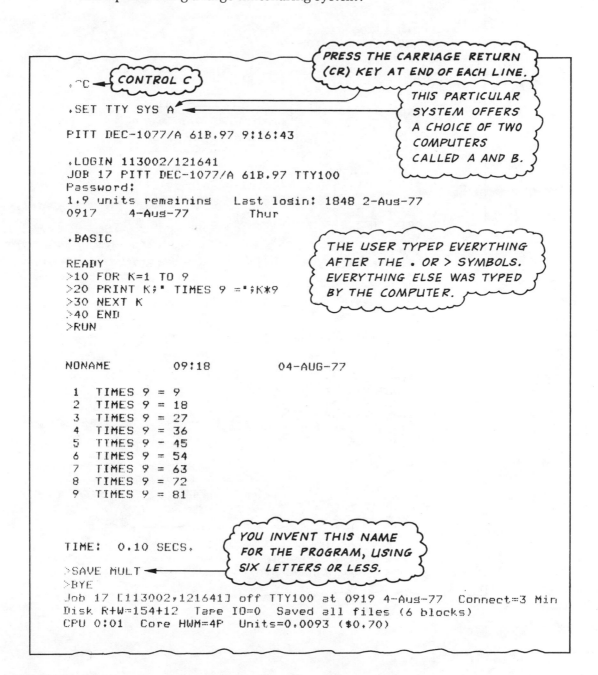

Example of a RUN on the same timesharing system some time later:

```
.SET TTY SYS A

PITT DEC-1077/A 61B.97 10:09:11

.LOGIN 113002/121641
JOB 19 PITT DEC-1077/A 61B.97 TTY100
Password:
1.9 units remaining   Last login: 0916 4-Aug-77
1009    4-Aug-77          Thur


.BASIC

>OLD MULT
>LIST


MULT              10:13           04-AUG-77

10 FOR K=1 TO 9
20 PRINT K;" TIMES 9 =";K*9
30 NEXT K
40 END
>5 PRINT"MULTIPLICATION TABLE FOR 9"
>RUN


MULT              10:14           04-AUG-77

MULTIPLICATION TABLE FOR 9
  1   TIMES 9 = 9
  2   TIMES 9 = 18
  3   TIMES 9 = 27
  4   TIMES 9 = 36
  5   TIMES 9 = 45
  6   TIMES 9 = 54
  7   TIMES 9 = 63
  8   TIMES 9 = 72
  9   TIMES 9 = 81



TIME:  0.12 SECS.
>REPLACE
>BYE
Job 19 [113002,121641] off TTY100 at 1014 4-Aug-77  Connect=6 Min
Disk R+W=153+43  Tape IO=0  Saved all files (12 blocks)
CPU 0:02  Core HWM=4P  Units=0.0124 ($0.93)
```

LOADS THE OLD "MULT" PROGRAM FROM DISK.

A NEW LINE IS PUT IN THE PROGRAM.

REPLACES THE OLD "MULT" PROGRAM ON DISK WITH THE NEW VERSION.

APPENDIX B: THE ASCII CODES

APPENDIX B 7-Bit ASCII Codes

Binary Form	Meaning of Code	Octal Form	Decimal Form
0000000	NULL (↑@)	000	0
0000001	SOH (↑A)	001	1
0000010	STX (↑B)	002	2
0000011	ETX (↑C)	003	3
0000100	EOT (↑D)	004	4
0000101	ENQ (↑E)	005	5
0000110	ACK (↑F)	006	6
0000111	BELL (↑G)	007	7
0001000	BS (↑H)	010	8
0001001	HT (↑I)	011	9
0001010	LF (↑J)	012	10
0001011	VT (↑K)	013	11
0001100	FF (↑L)	014	12
0001101	CR (↑M)	015	13
0001110	SO (↑N)	016	14
0001111	SI (↑O)	017	15
0010000	DLE (↑P)	020	16
0010001	DC1 (↑Q)	021	17
0010010	DC2 (↑R)	022	18
0010011	DC3 (↑S)	023	19
0010100	DC4 (↑T)	024	20
0010101	NAK (↑U)	025	21
0010110	SYN (↑V)	026	22
0010111	ETB (↑W)	027	23
0011000	CAN (↑X)	030	24
0011001	EM (↑Y)	031	25
0011010	SUB (↑Z)	032	26
0011011	ESC (↑[)	033	27
0011100	FS (↑\)	034	28
0011101	GS (↑])	035	29
0011110	RS (↑∧)	036	30
0011111	US (↑__)	037	31

Binary Form	Meaning of Code	Octal Form	Decimal Form
0100000	SP	040	32
0100001	!	041	33
0100010	"	042	34
0100011	#	043	35
0100100	$	044	36
0100101	%	045	37
0100110	&	046	38
0100111	'	047	39
0101000	(	050	40
0101001	)	051	41
0101010	*	052	42
0101011	+	053	43
0101100	,	054	44
0101101	—	055	45
0101110	.	056	46
0101111	/	057	47
0110000	0	060	48
0110001	1	061	49
0110010	2	062	50
0110011	3	063	51
0110100	4	064	52
0110101	5	065	53
0110110	6	066	54
0110111	7	067	55
0111000	8	070	56
0111001	9	071	57
0111010	:	072	58
0111011	;	073	59
0111100	<	074	60
0111101	=	075	61
0111110	>	076	62
0111111	?	077	63

Control Codes

The codes from octal 000 to octal 037 are used for special control functions. For example, code 002 is used in communications work to mean "start of text" (STX), while code 007 means "ring the bell on the terminal."

These codes do not print anything on output devices. However they can be sent to a computer in two ways.

(1) To input a control code from an ASCII keyboard, type the corresponding *control character* by holding down the key marked control

Binary Form	Meaning of Code	Octal Form	Decimal Form	Binary Form	Meaning of Code	Octal Form	Decimal Form
1000000	@	100	64	1100000	`	140	96
1000001	A	101	65	1100001	a	141	97
1000010	B	102	66	1100010	b	142	98
1000011	C	103	67	1100011	c	143	99
1000100	D	104	68	1100100	d	144	100
1000101	E	105	69	1100101	e	145	101
1000110	F	106	70	1100110	f	146	102
1000111	G	107	71	1100111	g	147	103
1001000	H	110	72	1101000	h	150	104
1001001	I	111	73	1101001	i	151	105
1001010	J	112	74	1101010	j	152	106
1001011	K	113	75	1101011	k	153	107
1001100	L	114	76	1101100	l	154	108
1001101	M	115	77	1101101	m	155	109
1001110	N	116	78	1101110	n	156	110
1001111	O	117	79	1101111	o	157	111
1010000	P	120	80	1110000	p	160	112
1010001	Q	121	81	1110001	q	161	113
1010010	R	122	82	1110010	r	162	114
1010011	S	123	83	1110011	s	163	115
1010100	T	124	84	1110100	t	164	116
1010101	U	125	85	1110101	u	165	117
1010110	V	126	86	1110110	v	166	118
1010111	W	127	87	1110111	w	167	119
1011000	X	130	88	1111000	x	170	120
1011001	Y	131	89	1111001	y	171	121
1011010	Z	132	90	1111010	z	172	122
1011011	[	133	91	1111011	{	173	123
1011100	\	134	92	1111100	|	174	124
1011101	]	135	93	1111101	}	175	125
1011110	∧	136	94	1111110	~	176	126
1011111	_	137	95	1111111	DEL	177	127

(CTRL), and then simultaneously pressing the character that has a code equal to the control code + 100 octal. For example, to ring the bell (code 007 octal) hold down the control key, and then simultaneously press the key for G (code 107 octal). Our table shows control-G as ↑G.

(2) To send a control code from BASIC, use the CHR$(D) function described in Section 4.7, where D is the *decimal* equivalent of the code. For example, to ring the bell use

10 PRINT CHR$(7)

On the Apple II this will produce a "beep" sound.

APPENDIX C:
SUMMARY OF BASIC

Statements

Name	Purpose	Example
(ln means line no.)		
DATA	Holds data for READ.	35 DATA 5,3.14,"SMITH"
DIM	Declares maximum size of array.	35 DIM A(15),X(20,4),N$(25)
END	Last statement in program.	9999 END
FOR...TO...(STEP)	Sets up and controls loop.	35 FOR K=1 TO N STEP 2
GOSUB ln	Branches to subroutine at ln.	35 GOSUB 800
GOTO ln	Branches to ln.	35 GOTO 55
IF...THEN ln	Branches to ln if condition true.	35 IF X-5<=2 THEN 125
IF...THEN stmts	Executes statements if true.	35 IF Z>5 THEN Z=1:PRINT Z
IF...THEN ln ELSE ln	Branches to first ln if true, branches to second ln if false.	35 IF Y=X THEN 85 ELSE 95
IF...THEN stmts ELSE stmts	Does stmts after THEN if true, does stmts after ELSE if false.	35 IF Y>M THEN M=Y ELSE N=Y:D=C
INPUT	Requests data from terminal.	35 INPUT A,B,N$
LET	Assigns value of expression to variable.	35 LET A=3.14*R*R
LINE INPUT	Inputs string containing commas,etc.	35 LINE INPUT A$
NEXT	Marks end of FOR loop.	35 NEXT K
ON X GOSUB...	Branches to Xth subroutine.	35 ON X GOSUB 899,999
ON Y GOTO...	Branches to Yth line number.	35 ON Y GOTO 65,75,85
PRINT	Types strings and/or numbers.	35 PRINT "ANS=";N+1.5,A$
PRINT USING	Types in given format.	35 PRINT USING "##.##";X
READ	Moves values from DATA into variables.	5 READ N,X,A$
RESTORE	Resets DATA pointer to first item.	35 RESTORE
RETURN	Go to statement following last GOSUB.	35 RETURN
STOP	Terminate program.	35 STOP

Special Features

POKE loc, val   PEEK (loc)   OUT port, val   PRINT @ N, exp

Commands

CLEAR, CONT, DELETE, EDIT, LIST, LOAD (CLOAD), NEW, OLD, RUN, SAVE (CSAVE)

Numeric Functions

Name	Purpose
ABS(X)	Absolute value of X
ATN(X)	Arctangent of X
COS(X)	Cosine of X
EXP(X)	e to the Xth power
INP(X)	Value at port X
INT(X)	Largest integer <= X
LOG(X)	Natural log of X
RND(1)	0 <= random number < 1
SGN(X)	Sign of X
SIN(X)	Sine of X
SQR(X)	Square root of X
TAN(X)	Tangent of X

String Functions

Name	Purpose
ASC(X$)	Decimal ASCII of 1st character in X$
CHR$(I)	Character with ASCII code I
INSTR(X$,Y$)	Position of Y$ in X$
LEFT$(X$,I)	Leftmost I characters of X$
LEN(X$)	Number of characters in X$
MID$(X$,I,J)	Substring of X$ starting at I with length J
RIGHT$(X$,I)	Rightmost I characters of X$
SPACE$(I)	String with I spaces
STR$(N)	String that looks like N
VAL(X$)	Number that looks like X$

Variables, Operators, Relations

A, Z, A1, Z9, X(I), X(I,J), N(X(I),K), A$, N$(I), Z$(I,J)

+,−,*,/,↑

<, <=, =, >=, >, <>

File Features

Vary with systems. See your system manual.

Index